Simple Latin Learning Resource for Newbies

Jody L. Martins

All rights reserved.

Copyright © 2024 Jody L. Martins

Simple Latin Learning Resource for Newbies : Easy Latin Mastery Guide for Beginners

Funny helpful tips:

Incorporate whole grains into your diet; they provide sustained energy and are rich in fiber.

Seek understanding over being right; harmony often trumps winning an argument.

Learn Latin For The Absolute Beginner

Ellena .H Coates

All rights reserved. Copyright © 2024 Ellena .H Coates

COPYRIGHT © 2024 Ellena .H Coates

All rights reserved.

No part of this book must be reproduced, stored in a retrieval system, or shared by any means, electronic, mechanical, photocopying, recording, or otherwise, without written permission from the publisher.

Every precaution has been taken in the preparation of this book; still the publisher and author assume no responsibility for errors or omissions. Nor do they assume any liability for damages resulting from the use of the information contained herein.

Legal Notice:

This book is copyright protected and is only meant for your individual use. You are not allowed to amend, distribute, sell, use, quote or paraphrase any of its part without the written consent of the author or publisher.

Introduction

This book offers a comprehensive introduction to the fundamentals of Latin grammar and vocabulary, making it an essential resource for students and enthusiasts alike. From cases and pronouns to verbs and vocabulary, each section of the book provides clear explanations and practical examples to help learners build a strong foundation in Latin language and culture.

The section on cases and abbreviations serves as a roadmap for navigating Latin grammar, highlighting the different grammatical cases and their functions within sentences. By understanding the role of each case, students can decode Latin texts more effectively and express themselves with precision.

Pronouns, possessive adjectives, and demonstrative pronouns are essential building blocks of Latin syntax, enabling learners to communicate ideas and relationships between objects and subjects. Through detailed explanations and exercises, students gain proficiency in using pronouns to convey meaning and clarity in their Latin compositions.

Relative and interrogative pronouns expand students' ability to ask questions, make comparisons, and establish connections between different parts of a sentence. With examples drawn from classical texts and everyday language, learners develop a nuanced understanding of how pronouns function in context.

Adiectivum, or adjectives, enrich students' descriptive vocabulary and enable them to express qualities and characteristics in their writing. With exercises that focus on adjective agreement and placement, learners develop the skills to craft vivid and nuanced descriptions in Latin prose and poetry.

The section on verb forms explores the conjugation patterns of regular and irregular verbs, empowering students to conjugate verbs accurately and use them in different tenses and moods. By mastering verb forms, learners unlock the power to express action, emotion, and intention in their Latin compositions.

Prepositions and adverbs provide additional tools for expressing relationships in Latin sentences, allowing students to convey spatial and temporal concepts with precision and clarity. By mastering these grammatical elements, learners can construct more sophisticated sentences and convey complex ideas with confidence.

Substantiva, or nouns, form the backbone of Latin vocabulary, encompassing a wide range of concepts and objects. Through extensive vocabulary lists and exercises, students acquire the words and phrases necessary for reading and understanding Latin texts across various genres and subjects.

In addition to grammar and syntax, Latin for Beginners provides insights into Latin culture and society through thematic vocabulary lists on topics such as greetings and farewells, professions and trades, countries and languages, and descriptions of people and animals. By engaging with these thematic units, students gain a deeper appreciation for the richness and diversity of Latin language and civilization.

With its comprehensive coverage of grammar, vocabulary, and culture, this book equips students with the tools they need to embark on a rewarding journey into the world of Latin language and literature, fostering a lifelong appreciation for the beauty and complexity of classical antiquity.

Contents

CASES AND ABBREVIATIONS 1
PRONOUNS 6
POSSESSIVE ADJECTIVES 9
DEMONSTRATIVE PRONOUNS 12
RELATIVE PRONOUNS 25
INTERROGATIVE PRONOUNS 26
PREPOSITIONS 35
ADVERBS 36
SUBSTANTIVA (NOUNS) 37
NOUNS 65
ADIECTIVUM (ADJECTIVES) 93
VERB FORMS IN LATIN 116
THE –ARE VERBS 118
THE –ERE VERBS 121
THE –IRE VERBS 126
IRREGULAR VERBS 127
VERBS (ALPHABETICAL LIST) 134
AD LUDUM (IN CLASS) 150
HOMINES (PEOPLE) 153
SALUTEM (GREETINGS AND FAREWELLS) 154
VERBA UTILIA (USEFUL WORDS ANDPHRASES) 156
FAM L A (THE FAM LY) 158
OFFICIIS (TRADES AND PROFESSIONS) 160
PATRIA (COUNTRIES) 164
LINGUAE MUNDI (LANGUAGES OF THEWORLD) 167
URBES (CITIES) 169
AETATE (TALKING ABOUT AGE) 171
DIES, MENSIS, ANNI TEMPUS (DAYS,MONTHS, SEASONS) 174
NUMERO (NUMBERS) 177
HORA DIEI (THE TIME OF DAY) 179

- ACT ONES (ACT V T ES) 181
- MANDUCARE ET BIBERE (EATING AND DRINKING) 189
- POPULUM DESCRIBERE (DESCRIBING PEOPLE) 194
- IN DOMO (AT HOME) 203
- TEMPESTAS (THE WEATHER) 206
- AN MAL A (AN MALS) 208
- NATURA (NATURE) 211
- TABLES 213

CASES AND ABBREVIATIONS

NOMINATIVE

The **nomimative case** refers to the *subject* of a sentence. For example:

Agricola puellae multam pecuniam dat.
The farmer gives the girl a lot of money.

In the above sentence, the word *argricola* (farmer) is the subject of the sentence.

ACCUSATIVE

The **accusative case** refers to the *direct object* in a sentence.

Agricola puellae multam pecuniam dat.
The farmer gives the girl a lot of money.

In the above sentence, the word *pecuniam* (money) is the direct object, because it receives the direct action of being given.

DATIVE

The **dative case** refers to the indirect object of the sentence.

Agricola puellae multam pecuniam dat.
The farmer gives the girl a lot of money.

In the above sentence, the word puellae (girl) is the indirect object, because she is the recipient of the direct object (the money).

GENITIVE

The **genitive case**, normally refers to possession (corresponding to the prepositions *of* and *from* in English).

ABLATIVE AND LOCATIVE

The **ablative** case expresses separation, indirection, or the means by which an action is performed. In English, the prepositions *by*, *with*, *from*, *in*, and *on* are most commonly used to indicate these meanings.

The **locative** case expresses the place where an action is performed. In early Latin the locative case had extensive use, but in Classical Latin the locative case was very rarely used, applying only to the names of cities and small islands and to a few other isolated words. For this purpose, the Romans considered all Mediterranean islands to be small except for Sicily, Sardinia, Corsica, Crete, and Cyprus. Much of the case's function had been absorbed into the ablative. In the first and second declension singular, the locative is identical to the genitive singular, and in the third declension singular it is identical to the dative singular. For plural nouns of all declensions, the locative is also identical to the ablative. The few fourth- and fifth-declension place names would also use the ablative form for the locative case. However, a few nouns use the locative instead of a preposition: bellum → bellī 'at war'; domus → domī 'at home'; rūs → rūrī 'in the country'; humus → humī 'on the ground'; mīlitia → mīlitiae 'in military service, in the field'; focus → focī 'at the hearth', 'at the center of the community'. In archaic times, the locative singular of third declension nouns was interchangeable between the ablative and dative but, in the Augustan period, the use of the dative became fixed.*

*https://en.wikipedia.org/wiki/Latin_declension#Meanings_and_functions_of_the_various_cases

VOCATIVE

The vocative case refers to directly address a person (or something even a thing). Often, in English literature and poetry we express the same using "O" or "Oh" (for example: "Oh grave, where is thy victory? Oh death, where is thy sting?" Here some examples:

Quid fecit, senatores?
What are you doing, Senators?

Et tu, mi fili Brute?
And you, too, Brutus, my child?

Quo vadis, Marce?
Where are you going, Marcus?

Quid facis, mi fili?
What are you doing, my son?

CASES AND SYNTAX

The syntax in Latin is much more flexible than the syntax in English, since the case ending (declension) of the word indicates its place in the sentence. For example:

Agricola puellae multam pecuniam dat.
The farmer gives the girl a lot of money.

In the above sentence literally translates:

The farmer to the girl much money gives.

However, you could easily change the word order to say:

Much money the farmer to the girl gives.

or

To the girl much money the farmer gives.

In English, using alternative word orders seems strange or other times could impede properly understanding the meaning of the sentence. However in Latin, the meaning is always clear due to the case endings.

Please note that in Latin, the verb (*dat* in this case) often comes at the end of sentence, as in the example we have chosen:

Agricola puellae multam pecuniam dat.
The farmer gives the girl a lot of money.

ABBREVIATIONS

m. – mascuiline

f. – feminine

n. – neuter

sing. – singular

pl. - plural

Abl – Ablative Case

Acc – Accusative Case

Dat – Dative Case

Decl – Declension

Gen – Genitive Case

Conj – Conjugation

Nom – Nomative Case

Voc – Vocative Case

PRONOUNS

SINGULAR

ego – I
mei – of me, from me
me – me (direct obj.)
mihi – to me

tu – you
tui – of you, from you
te – you (direct obj.)
tibi – to you

is – he
eius – of him, from him
eum – him (direct obj.)
ei – to him
sui/sibi/se – himself*

ea – she
eius – of her, from her
eam – her (direct obj.)
ei – to her
sui/sibi/se – herself*

id – it
eius – of it, from it
id – it (direct obj.)
ei – to it
sui/sibi/se – itself*

*reflexive

OVERVIEW WITH TABLE

SINGULAR	I	you	he	she	it
NOM	ego	tu	is	ea	id
GEN	mei	tui	eius	eius	eius
DAT	mihi	tibi	ei	ei	ei
ACC	me	te	eum	eam	id
ABL	me(cum)	te(cum)	eo	ea	eo

PLURAL

nos – we
nostrum/nostri – of us, from us
nos – us (direct obj.)
nobis – to us

vos – you
vestrum/vestri – of you, from you
vos – you (direct obj.)
vobis – to you

ei/ii – they (m.)
eorum – of them, from them (m.)
eos – them (direct obj.)
eis – to them (m.)

eae – they (f.)
earum – of them, from them (f.)
eas – them (direct obj.)
eis – to them (f.)

ea – they (n.)
eorum – of them, from them (n.)
ea – them (direct obj.)

eis – to them (n.)

OVERVIEW WITH TABLE

PLURAL	we	you	they (m.)	they (f.)	they (n.)
NOM	nos	vos	ei/ii	eae	ea
GEN	nostri nostrum	vestri vestrum	eorum	earum	eorum
DAT	nobis	vobis	eis	eis	eis
ACC	nos	vos	eos	eas	ea
ABL	nobis(cum)	vobis(cum)	eis	eis	eis

POSSESSIVE ADJECTIVES

MEUS (MY)

meus, mea, meum – my

Vulnerasti cor meum soror mea sponsa vulnerasti cor meum in uno oculorum tuorum et in uno crine colli tui.

You have ravished my heart, my sister, my bride, you have ravished my heart with one of your eyes and one chain (curl) of your neck.

Vulgate, Song of Solomon 4:9

TUUS (YOUR - SINGULAR)

tuus, tua(m), tuo, tuum – your

Ubi est fratus tuus?
Where is your brother?[1]

Ubi est Sara uxor tua?
Where is Sara, your wife?[2]

Et ei qui vult tecum iudicio contendere et tunicam tuam tollere remitte ei et pallium.
And if a man takes you to court to take your coat, give him also your cloak.[3]

Cur temptavit Satanas cor tuum?
Why has Satan tempted your heart?[4]

Quare posuisti in corde tuo hanc rem?
Why have you conceived this thing in your heart?[4]

[1]*Vulgate*, Gen. 4:9
[2]*Vulgate*, Gen. 18:9
[3]*Vulgate*, Matt. 5:40
[4]*Vulgate*, Acts 5: 3,4

EIUS/ILLIUS/SUUS (HIS, HER, ITS)

eius/illius/suus, sui – his, her, its

Manus illius tornatiles aureae plenae hyacinthis. Venter eius eburneus distinctus sapphyris.

His hands are as gold rings set with the beryl: His belly is as bright ivory overlaid with sapphires.– *Vulgate*, Song of Solomon 5:14

Et cassis aerea super caput eius et lorica hamata induebatur porro pondus loricae eius quinque milia siclorum aeris. Et ocreas aereas habebat in cruribus et clypeus aereus tegebat umeros eius.

And he had an helmet of brass upon his head, and he was armed with a coat of mail; and the weight of the coat was five thousand shekels of brass. On his legs he wore bronze greaves, and a bronze shield was slung on his back.– *Vulgate*, 1 Samuel 17:5,6

NOSTER (OUR)

noster, nostra, nostrum – our

Pater noster qui in caelis es sanctificetur nomen tuum.
Our father, who are in heaven, hallowed be your name.

Panem nostrum supersubstantialem da nobis hodie.
Give us this day our daily bread.

-*Vulgate*, Matthew 6:9,11

Et quomodo nos audivimus unusquisque lingua nostra in qua nati sumus?
And how is it that we hear each one of us in our mother tongue? (lit. in the language where we were born) – *Vulgate*, Acts 2:8

VESTER (YOUR - PLURAL)

vester, vestra, vestrum – your (plural)

Scit enim pater vester quibus opus sit vobis antequam petatis eum.
For your father knows what you need before you ask him -*Vulgate*, Matt. 6:8

EORUM (THEIR)

eorum, earum, eorum – their

Amant filium eorum.
Filium eorum amant.
They love their son.

DEMONSTRATIVE PRONOUNS

HIC, HAEC, HOC: (THIS, THESE)

MASCULINE

this, these

Masculine	Singular	Plural
Nom	hic	hi
Gen	huius	horum
Dat	huic	his
Acc	hunc	hos
Abl	hoc	his

<u>Singular</u>
Nom: hic
Gen: huius
Dat: huic
Acc: hunc
Abl: hoc

<u>Plural</u>
Nom: hi
Gen: horum
Dat: his
Acc: hos
Abl: his

Quid *hic* sic loquitur?
Why does this (man) speak thus?

—*Vulgate*, Mark 2:7

FEMININE

this, these

Feminine	Singular	Plural
Nom	haec	hae
Gen	huius	harum
Dat	huic	his
Acc	hanc	has
Abl	hac	his

<u>Singular</u>
Nom: haec
Gen: huius
Dat: huic
Acc: hanc
Abl: hac

<u>Plural</u>
Nom: hae
Gen: harum
Dat: his
Acc: has
Abl: his

Quare posuisti in corde tuo hanc rem?
Why have you conceived this thing in your heart?

-*Vulgate* Acts 5:4

NEUTER

this, these

Neuter	Singular	Plural
Nom	hoc	haec
Gen	huius	horum
Dat	huic	his
Acc	hoc	haec
Abl	hoc	his

Singular
Nom: hoc
Gen: huius
Dat: huic
Acc: hoc
Abl: hoc

Plural
Nom: haec
Gen: horum
Dat: his
Acc: haec
Abl: his

Quidnam est hoc?
What is this?

OVERVIEW (TABLES)

this

Masculine	Singular	Plural
Nom	hic	hi
Gen	huius	horum
Dat	huic	his
Acc	hunc	hos
Abl	hoc	his

Feminine	Singular	Plural
Nom	haec	hae
Gen	huius	harum
Dat	huic	his
Acc	hanc	has
Abl	hac	his

Neuter	Singular	Plural
Nom	hoc	haec
Gen	huius	horum
Dat	huic	his
Acc	hoc	haec
Abl	hoc	his

ISTE, ISTA, ISTUD: (THIS/THAT, THESE/THOSE)

MASCULINE

this/that, these/those

Masculine	Singular	Plural
Nom	iste	isti
Gen	istius	istorum
Dat	isti	istis
Acc	istum	istos
Abl	isto	istis

Singular
Nom: iste
Gen: istius
Dat: isti
Acc: istum
Abl: isto

Plural
Nom: isti
Gen: istorum
Dat: istis
Acc: istos
Abl: istis

FEMININE

this/that, these/those

Feminine	Singular	Plural
Nom	ista	istae
Gen	istius	istarum
Dat	isti	istis
Acc	istam	istas
Abl	ista	istis

<u>Singular</u>
Nom: ista
Gen: istius
Dat: isti
Acc: istam
Abl: ista

<u>Plural</u>
Nom: istae
Gen: istarum
Dat: istis
Acc: istas
Abl: istis

Quid ista cogitatis?
Why do you think that?

Quando ista fient?
When will that happen?
When will this come to pass?

NEUTER

this/that, these/those

Neuter	Singular	Plural
Nom	istud	ista
Gen	istius	istorum
Dat	isti	istis
Acc	istud	ista
Abl	isto	istis

Singular
Nom: istud
Gen: istius
Dat: isti
Acc: istud
Abl: isto

Plural
Nom: ista
Gen: istorum
Dat: istis
Acc: ista
Abl: istis

OVERVIEW (TABLES)

that, those

Masculine	Singular	Plural
Nom	iste	isti
Gen	istius	istorum
Dat	isti	istis
Acc	istum	istos
Abl	isto	istis

Feminine	Singular	Plural
Nom	ista	istae
Gen	istius	istarum
Dat	isti	istis
Acc	istam	istas
Abl	ista	istis

Neuter	Singular	Plural
Nom	istud	ista
Gen	istius	istorum
Dat	isti	istis
Acc	istud	ista
Abl	isto	istis

ILLE, ILLA, ILLUD (THAT, THOSE)

Please note that in Latin, there is no word that corresponds to the definite article "the" in English. For example:

magna tunica
a big coat
the big coat

Often times in Latin a demonstrative word can also be used in place of the definite article "the" in English. For example:

illa magna tunica
the big coat
(literally "that big coat")

Please also notice that in Latin, demonstratives are often used in place of personal pronouns. For example

is = he

Honestus est.
He is honest. (the pronoun "is" is omitted)

Ille honestus est.
He is honest. ("ille" instead of "is")
(literally "That one is honest")

MASCULINE

that, those

Masculine	Singular	Plural
Nom	ille	illi
Gen	illius	illorum
Dat	illi	illis
Acc	illum	illos
Abl	illo	illis

Singular
Nom: ille
Gen: illius
Dat: illi
Acc: illum
Abl: illo

Plural
Nom: illi
Gen: illorum
Dat: illis
Acc: illos
Abl: illis

FEMININE

that, those

Feminine	Singular	Plural
Nom	illa	illae
Gen	illius	illarum
Dat	illi	illis
Acc	illam	illas
Abl	illa	illis

<u>Singular</u>
Nom: illa
Gen: illius
Dat: illi
Acc: illam
Abl: illa

<u>Plural</u>
Nom: illae
Gen: illarum
Dat: illis
Acc: illas
Abl: illis

NEUTER

that, those

Neuter	Singular	Plural
Nom	illud	illa
Gen	illius	illorum
Dat	illi	illis
Acc	illud	illa
Abl	illo	illis

<u>Singular</u>
Nom: illud
Gen: illius
Dat: illi
Acc: illud
Abl: illo

<u>Plural</u>
Nom: illa
Gen: illorum
Dat: illis
Acc: illa
Abl: illis

RELATIVE PRONOUNS

that, which, who, whose, etc.

SING	M	F	N
NOM	qui	quae	quod
GEN	cuius	cuius	cuius
DAT	cui	cui	cui
ACC	quem	quam	quod
ABL	quo	qua	quo

PLURAL	M	F	N
NOM	qui	quae	quae
GEN	quorum	quarum	quorum
DAT	quibus	quibus	quibus
ACC	quos	quas	quae
ABL	quibus	quibus	quibus

INTERROGATIVE PRONOUNS

Who?, What?, Which?, Why?

SING	M	F	N
NOM	quis	quis	quid
GEN	cuius	cuius	cuius
DAT	cui	cui	cui
ACC	quem	quem	quid
ABL	quo	quo	quo

PLURAL	M	F	N
NOM	qui	quae	quae
GEN	quorum	quarum	quorum
DAT	quibus	quibus	quibus
ACC	quos	quas	quae
ABL	quibus	quibus	quibus

EXAMPLES

QUID, QUIS AND QUI

Quid agis?/Quid facis?
What are you doing?

Quid facitis?
What are you (all) doing?

Quid est facilius?
Which is easier?

Quid petam?
What shall I ask for?

Quidnam est hoc?
What is that?
Which thing is that ?

Quis es?
Who are you?

Qui estis?
Who are you all?

Qui sunt?
Who are they?

Quid hic sic loquitur?
Why does this man speak thus?
-*Vulgate*, Mark 2:7

Quid ista cogitatis?
Why do you think that?*

*There are other words which can translate "why" in Latin. For example:

quare?

Quare posuisti in corde tuo hanc rem?
Why have you conceived this thing in your heart?

cur?

Cur temptavit Satanas cor tuum?
Why has Satan tempted your heart?

-Vulgate, Acts 5:3, 4

UBI, UNDE, QUO

Ubi es?
Where are you?

Ubi est fratus tuus?
Where is your brother?

Ubi est Sara uxor tua?
Where is Sarah your wife?

Ubi sunt viri?
Where are the men?

Ubi habitas?
Where do you live?

Unde venis?
Where do you come from?

Unde venistis?
Where have you come from?

Quo vadis?
Where are you going?

QUOMODO

quomodo (how?)

Quomodo potest homo nasci cum senex sit?
How can a man be born again when he is old?

- *Vulgate*, John 3:4

Et quomodo nos audivimus unusquisque lingua nostra in qua nati sumus?
And how is it that we hear each one of us in our mother tongue? (lit. in the language where we were born) – *Vulgate*, Acts 2:8

QUANDO

quando (when?)

Quando ista fient?
When will that come to pass?
When will this happen?

EXAMPLES FROM THE LATIN VULGATE

Gen. 3:9-13 – And the Lord called to Adam "Where are you?"
Vocavitque Dominus Deus Adam et dixit ei "Ubi es?"

Qui ait vocem tuam audivi in paradiso et timui eo quod nudus essem et abscondi me

Who answered him: "I heard your voice in paradise, and I was afraid because I was naked and I hid myself."

Cui dixit "quis enim indicavit tibi quod nudus esses nisi quod ex ligno de quo tibi praeceperam ne comederes comedisti?"

And he said to him: And who hath told thee that thou wast naked, but that thou hast eaten of the tree whereof I commanded thee that thou shouldst not eat?

Et dixit Dominus Deus ad mulierem "quare hoc fecisti?" quae respondit serpens decepit me et comedi.

And the Lord God said to the woman: Why hast thou done this? And she answered: The serpent deceived me, and I did eat.

Gen. 4:6-9
Dixitque Dominus ad eum "quare maestus es? et cur concidit facies tua?

And the Lord said to him: Why art thou angry? and why is thy countenance fallen?

Et ait Dominus ad Cain ubi est Abel frater tuus qui respondit nescio num custos fratris mei sum?

And the Lord said to Cain: Where is thy brother Abel? And he answered, I know not: am I my brother's keeper?

Gen. 16:8
Dixit ad eam Agar ancilla Sarai "unde venis et quo vadis?" quae respondit a facie Sarai dominae meae ego fugio.

He said to her: Agar, handmaid of Sarai, whence comest thou? and whither goest thou? And she answered: I flee from the face of Sarai, my mistress

Gen. 18:9
Cumque comedissent dixerunt ad eum ubi est Sara uxor tua ille respondit ecce in tabernaculo est.

And when they had eaten, they said to him: Where is Sara thy wife? He answered: Lo, she is in the tent.

Gen.19:5
Vocaveruntque Loth et dixerunt ei "ubi sunt viri qui introierunt ad te nocte?" educ illos huc ut cognoscamus eos.

And they called Lot, and said to him: Where are the men that came in to thee at night? bring them out hither that we may know them.

Gen. 21:17, 29
Exaudivit autem Deus vocem pueri vocavitque angelus Domini Agar de caelo dicens "quid agis Agar?" noli timere exaudivit enim Deus vocem pueri de loco in quo est.

And God heard the voice of the boy: and an angel of God called to Agar from heaven, saying: What art thou doing, Agar? fear not: for God hath heard the voice of the boy, from the place wherein he is.

Cui dixit Abimelech "quid sibi volunt septem agnae istae quas stare fecisti seorsum?"

And Abimelech said to him: What mean these seven ewe lambs which thou hast set apart?

Gen. 24:23
Cuius es filia?
Whose daughter are you?

Gen. 24:31 *Cur foris stas?*
Why are you standing outside?

Gen. 24:39
Ego vero respondi domino meo "quid si noluerit venire mecum mulier?

But I answered my master: What if the woman will not come with me?

Gen. 24:65
Et ait ad puerum "quis est ille homo qui venit per agrum in occursum nobis?" dixit ei ipse est dominus meus at illa tollens cito pallium operuit se.

And said to the servant: Who is that man who cometh towards us along the field? And he said to her: That man is my master. But she quickly took her cloak, and covered herself.

Gen. 26:9, 27
Et accersito ait perspicuum est quod uxor tua sit "cur mentitus es sororem tuam?" esse respondit timui ne morerer propter eam.

And calling for him, he said: It is evident she is thy wife: why didst thou feign her to be thy sister? He answered: I feared lest I should die for her sake.

Locutus est eis Isaac "quid venistis ad me hominem quem odistis et expulistis a vobis?"

Isaac said to them: Why are ye come to me, a man whom you hate, and have thrust out from you?

Gen. 27:20

Rursum Isaac ad filium suum "quomodo inquit tam cito invenire potuisti fili mi?" qui respondit voluntatis Dei fuit ut cito mihi occurreret quod volebam.

And Isaac said to his son: How couldst thou find it so quickly, my son? He answered: It was the will of God, that what I sought came quickly in my way:

Gen. 29:4-6

Dixitque ad pastores fratres "unde estis?" qui responderunt de Haran.

And he said to the shepherds: Brethren, whence are you? They answered: Of Haran.

Quos interrogans numquid ait "nostis Laban filium Nahor?" dixerunt novimus.

And he asked them, saying: Know you Laban the son of Nachor? They said: We know him.

"sanusne est?" inquit valet inquiunt et ecce Rahel filia eius venit cum grege suo.

He said: Is he in health? He is in health, say they: and behold Rachel his daughter cometh with his flock.

Gen. 29: 25
Et dixit ad socerum "quid est quod facere voluisti? nonne pro Rahel servivi tibi? quare inposuisti mihi?"

And he said to his father in law: What is it that thou didst mean to do? did not I serve thee for Rachel? why hast thou deceived me?

Gen. 30: 31

Dixitque Laban "quid dabo tibi?" at ille ait nihil volo sed si feceris quod postulo iterum pascam et custodiam pecora tua.

And Laban said: What shall I give thee? But he said: I require nothing: but if thou wilt do what I demand, I will feed, and keep thy sheep again.

PREPOSITIONS

Here is an alphabetical list of prepositions in Latin. You have in parentheses the case which this preposition requires (or with which it is used):

abb – Ablative Case

acc – Accusative Case

A/Ab (abb) — from, away from
Ad (acc) — to, towards, near to
Ante (acc) — before
Apud (acc) — next to, at
Circum (acc) — around
Contra (acc) — against, in opposition of
Cum (abb) — with (in the company of)
De (abb) — from
E/Ex (abb) — from, out of, out from
Extra (acc) — outside
In (abb or acc) — into or against (acc), in, on or among (abb)
Inter (acc) — among, between
Ob (acc) — in the way of, against, on account of
Per (acc) — through
Post (acc) — behind, after
Pro (abb) — for, on behalf of
Propter (acc) — on account of, because of
Sine (acc) — without
Sub (abb or acc) — under
Super (acc) — above
Trans (acc) — across

ADVERBS

<u>adverbs</u>
ad detrix – at the right (side)
ad dexteram – on the right hand
ad sinistram – on the left hand
ad vesperam – in the evening
nunc – now
nunquam – never
Numquam sic vidimus! – We never saw anything like that!

iterum – again, a second time, repeatedly

nihil – nothing
pauci – a few
semper – always, ever
saepe – often
si – if
si vis – if you wish
si vis potes – if you wish you can
cum - with
sine - without

ibi – here

SUBSTANTIVA (NOUNS)

THE FIRST DECLENSION
(a-Declension)

Most nouns in this declension which end with an -a are feminine with the following exceptions: *agricola* (farmer), *athleta* (athlete), *nauta* (sailor), *poeta* (poet), pirata (pirate) and *scriba* (scribe, secretary).

<u>Singular</u>
Nom: domin**a**
Gen: domin**ae**
Dat: domin**ae**
Acc: domin**am**
Abl: domin**a**
Voc: domin**a**

<u>Plural</u>
Nom: domin**ae**
Gen: domin**arum**
Dat: domin**is**
Acc: domin**as**
Abl: domin**is**
Voc: domin**ae**

THE NOUN DOMINA (F.) "LADY, MISTRESS"

First Decl	Singular	Plural
Nom	domina	dominae
Gen	dominae	dominarum
Dat	dominae	dominis
Acc	dominam	dominas

| Abl | domina | dominis |
| Voc | domina | dominae |

THE NOUN NAUTA (M.) "SAILOR"

First Decl	Singular	Plural
Nom	nauta	nautae
Gen	nautae	nautarum
Dat	nautae	nautis
Acc	nautam	nautas
Abl	nauta	nautis
Voc	nauta	nautae

LIST OF NOUNS FROM THE FIRST DECLENSION

agricola – farmer
athleta – athlete
aranea – spider
aqua – water
barba – beard
cathedra – seat, chair
causa – cause
culpa – guilt
fama – fame, renown, report, rumor
femina – woman
forma – form
fortuna – fortune, happiness
gloria – glory, fame, honor
ira – anger, wrath
lorica – coat, coat of mail
mensa – table

mora – delay, wait
musca – fly
nauta – sailor, sea man
patria – country, nation
pecunia – money
philosophia – philosophy
poena – penalty, punishment, pain
pirata – pirate
poeta – poet
porta – gate
puella – girl
rosa – rose
schola – school
scriba – scribe, secretary
sella – seat, chair
terra – earth
tunica – shirt, coat, jacket
turba – crowd
villa – village
vita – life

THE SECOND DECLENSION
(o-Declension)

THE NOUN DOMINUS (M.) "THE LORD"

2nd Decl	Singular	Plural
Nom	dominus	domini
Gen	domini	dominorum
Dat	domino	dominis
Acc	dominum	dominos
Abl	domino	dominis
Voc	domine	domini

<u>Singular</u>
Nom: domin**us**
Gen: domin**i**
Dat: domin**o**
Acc: domin**um**
Abl: domin**o**
Voc: domin**e**

<u>Plural</u>
Nom: domin**i**
Gen: domin**orum**
Dat: domin**is**
Acc: domin**os**
Abl: domin**is**
Voc: domin**i**

OTHER NOUNS LIKE "DOMINUS"

amicus – friend

animus – soul, spirit
cervus – deer
filius – son
gallus – rooster, cockerel
(h)umerus – shoulder
murus – wall
musculus – muscle
nasus – nose
oculus – eye
numerus – number
populus – people
pullus – chicken
porcus – pig

THE NOUN PUER (M.) "aOy"

2nd Decl	Singular	Plural
Nom	puer	pueri
Gen	pueri	puerorum
Dat	puero	pueris
Acc	puerum	pueros
Abl	puero	pueris
Voc	puer	pueri

Singular
Nom: pu**er**
Gen: puer**i**
Dat: puer**o**
Acc: peur**um**
Abl: peur**o**
Voc: peur

Plural
Nom: peur**i**
Gen: peur**orum**
Dat: peur**is**
Acc: peur**os**
Abl: peur**is**
Voc: peur**i**

THE NOUN AGER (M.) "FIELD"

2nd Decl	Singular	Plural
Nom	ager	agri
Gen	agri	agrorum
Dat	agro	agris
Acc	agrum	agros
Abl	agro	agris
Voc	ager	agri

<u>Singular</u>
Nom: ager
Gen: agri
Dat: agro
Ac: agrum
Abl: agro
Voc: ager

<u>Plural</u>
Nom: agri
Gen: agrorum
Dat: agris
Acc: agros
Abl: agris
Voc: agri

OTHER NOUNS LJKE "PUER" AND "AGER"

arbiter, *arbitri* – judge
cancer, *cancri* – crab
caper, *capri* – male goat
culter, *cultri* – knife

faber, *fabri* – smith, carpenter
liber, *libri* – book
magister, *magistri* – teacher, master
minister, *ministri* – server, servant, minister
vir, *viri* – man

THE NOUN TEMPLUM (N.) "TEMPLE"

Some nouns in the second declesion are neuter. For example:

templum (temple)

2nd Decl	Singular	Plural
Nom	templum	templa
Gen	templi	templorum
Dat	templo	templis
Acc	templum	templa
Abl	tempo	templis
Voc	templum	templa

<u>Singular</u>
Nom: templ**um**
Gen: templ**i**
Dat: templ**o**
Acc: templ**um**
Abl: templ**o**
Voc: templ**um**

<u>Plural</u>
Nom: templ**a**
Gen: templ**orum**
Dat: templ**is**
Acc: templ**a**
Abl: templ**is**
Voc: templ**a**

OTHER NOUNS LIKE "TEMPLUM"

basium – kiss

brachium – arm
bellum – war
caelum – sky
cerebrum – brain
collum – neck
donum – gift
odium – hate
officium – office, function, duty
pallium – cloak, cape
otium – leisure, freetime
periculum – danger
vinum – wine
vitium – vice, defect

Magnum bellum volo.
I want a big war.

Magnum bellum nolo.
I don't want a big war.

Bella sunt mala.
Wars are bad.

Omnia bella stulta sunt.
All wars are foolish.

THE THIRD DECLENSION

The third declension is the largest group of nouns. The nominative singular of these nouns may end in -a, -e, -ī, -ō, -y, -c, -l, -n, -r, -s, -t, or -x. This group of nouns includes masculine, neuter, and feminine nouns. Examples are *flūmen, flūminis* n. ('river'), *flōs, flōris* m. ('flower'), and *pāx, pācis* f. ('peace'). Each noun has the ending *-is* as a suffix attached to the root of the noun in the genitive singular form. Masculine, feminine and neuter nouns each have their own special nominative singular endings. For instance, many masculine nouns end in *-or* (*amor, amōris*, 'love'). Many feminine nouns end in *-īx* (*phoenīx, phoenīcis*, 'phoenix'), and many neuter nouns end in *-us* with an *r* stem in the oblique cases (*onus, oneris* 'burden'; *tempus, temporis* 'time').

https://en.wikipedia.org/wiki/Latin_declension#Third_declension_(i_and_consonant_stems)

MASCULINE AND FEMININE

Singular
Nom: --*
Gen: –is
Dat: –i
Acc: –em
Abl: –e

Plural
Nom: –es
Gen: –um
Dat: –ibus
Acc: –es

Abl: –ibus

*This ending is unique for each noun. For example:

amor (love)
homo (man)
pater (father)
vox (voice)

THE NOUN PATER (M.) "FATHER"

3rd Decl	Singular	Plural
Nom	pater	patres
Gen	patris	patrum
Dat	patri	patribus
Acc	patrem	patres
Abl	patre	partibus
Voc	pater	patres

Singular
pater
patris
patri
patrem
patre

Plural
patres
patrum
patribus
patres
patribus

Here are other masculine nouns like "pater":

amor, *amoris* (love)
homo, *hominis* (man)
labor, *laboris* (work)
rex, *regis* (king)

THE NOUN VOX (F.) "VOICE"

3rd Decl	Singular	Plural
Nom	vox	voces
Gen	vocis	vocum
Dat	voci	vocibus
Acc	vocem	voces
Abl	voce	vocibus
Voc	vox	voces

<u>Singular</u>
Nom: vox
Gen: vocis
Dat: voci
Acc: vocem
Abl: voce

<u>Plural</u>
Nom: voces
Gen: vocum
Dat: vocibus
Acc: voces
Abl: vocibus

NEUTER

THE NOUN NOMEN (N.) "NAME"

3rd Decl	Singular	Plural
Nom	nomen	nomina
Gen	nominis	nominum
Dat	nomini	nominibus
Acc	nomen	nomina
Abl	nomine	nominibus
Voc	nomen	nomina

Singular
nomen
nominis
nomini
nomen
nomine

Plural
nomina
nominum
nominibus
nomina
nominibus

THE NOUN CORPUS (N.) "aOoy"

3rd Decl	Singular	Plural
Nom	corpus	corpora
Gen	corporis	corpurum
Dat	corpori	corporibus
Acc	corpus	corpora
Abl	corpore	corporibus

Singular
corpus
corporis
corpori
corpus
corpore

Plural
corpora
corporum
corporibus
corpora
corporibus

Other nouns like "corpus":

h(olus) (vegetables)
pondus (weight, force)
tempus (time)

THE I-STEM DECLENSION

Third declension i-stem nouns[edit]

The third declension also has a set of nouns that are declined differently. They are called i-stems. i-stems are broken into two subcategories: pure and mixed. Pure i-stems are indicated by the parisyllabic rule or special neuter endings. Mixed i-stems are indicated by the double consonant rule.

Masculine and feminine

Parisyllabic rule: Some masculine and feminine third-declension i-stem nouns have the same number of syllables in the genitive as they do in the nominative. For example: amnis, amnis ('stream'). The nominative ends in -is.

Double consonant rule: The rest of the masculine and feminine third-declension i-stem nouns have two consonants before the -is in the genitive singular. For example: pars, partis ('part').

Neuter

Special neuter ending: Neuter third-declension i-stems have no rule. However, all of them end in -al, -ar or -e. For example: animal, animālis ('animal'); cochlear, cochleāris ('spoon'); mare, maris ('sea').

https://en.wikipedia.org/wiki/Latin_declension#Third_declension_(i_and_consonant_stems)

MASCULINE AND FEMININE
THE NOUN NOX (F.) "NIGHT"

3rd Decl	Singular	Plural
Nom	nox	noctes
Gen	noctis	noctium
Dat	nocti	noctibus
Acc	noctem	noctes
Abl	nocte	noctibus
Voc	nox	noctes

Singular
nox
noctis
nocti
noctem
nocte

Plural
noctes
noctium
noctibus
noctes
noctibus

Here are other nouns like "nox":

Masculine
civis, civis – citizen
dens, dentis – tooth

Feminine
ars, artis – art, skill

civis, civis – citizen
finis, finis – end
mors, mortis – death
navis, navis – ship
pars, partis – part
urbs, urbis – city

NEUTER

THE NOUN MARE (N.) "SEA"

3rd Decl	Singular	Plural
Nom	mare	maria
Gen	maris	marium
Dat	mari	maribus
Acc	mare	maria
Abl	mari	maribus
Voc	mare	maria

Here is another noun like "mare":

animal, animalis – animal

NOUNS LIKE TURRIS (F.) "TOWER"

There are also nouns like the noun *turris* (tower). For example:

turris (f.) "tower"

3rd Decl	Singular	Plural
Nom	turris	turres
Gen	turris	turrium
Dat	turri	turribus
Acc	turrim	turres
Abl	turri	turribus

Singular
turris
turris
turri
turrim
turri

Plural
turres
turrium
turribus
turris/turres
turribus

Here are other nouns of this declension, like the noun *turris*:

cassis (helm)
febris (fever)
pelvis (pelvis)
restis (string, rope)

57

securis (axe)
sitis (thirst)
tussis (cough)
vis (force)

THE FOURTH DECLENSION

Most nouns of the fourth declension with the nominative singular ending in -us are masculine, for example casus "case". Exceptions are, for example, the feminine *domus* ("house") and *manus* "hand". There are also neuter nouns like *genu* "knee" and *cornu* "horn".

THE NOUN FRUCTUS (M.) "FRUIT"

4th Decl	Singular	Plural
Nom	fructus	fructus
Gen	fructus	fructuum
Dat	fructui	fructibus
Acc	fructum	fructus
Abl	fructu	fructibus

Singular
Nom: fructus
Gen: fructus
Dat: fructui
Acc: fructum
Abl: fructu

Plural
Nom: fructus
Gen: fructuum
Dat: fructibus
Acc: fructus
Abl: fructibus

Here are some other masculine nouns:

casus (case)
metus (fear)

Senatus (Senate)
versus (verse)

There are also feminine nouns which are declined like *fructus*:

domus (house, home)
manus (hand)
servitus (slavery)

THE NOUN CORNU (N.) "HORN"

4th Decl	Singular	Plural
Nom	cornu	cornua
Gen	cornus	cornuum
Dat	cornu	cornibus
Acc	cornu	cornua
Abl	cornu	cornibus

Singular
Nom: cornu
Gen: cornus
Dat: cornu
Acc: cornu
Abl: cornu

Plural
Nom: cornua
Gen: cornuum
Dat: cornibus
Acc: cornua
Abl: cornibus

THE FIFTH DECLENSION

Virtually all nouns of the fifth declension are feminine, for example *res* (thing), with the exception of the masculine noun *dies* (day). There are no neuter nouns in this declension.

THE NOUN RES (F.) "THING", "MATTER"

5th Decl	Singular	Plural
Nom	res	res
Gen	rei	rerum
Dat	rei	rebus
Acc	rem	res
Abl	re	rebus

Singular
Nom: res
Gen: rei
Dat: rei
Acc: rem
Abl: re

Plural
Nom: res
Gen: rerum
Dat: rebus
Acc: res
Abl: rebus

For example:

Quare posuisti in corde tuo hanc rem?
Why have you conceived this thing in your heart?

Here are some other feminine nouns:

fides (faith)
spes (hope)

THE NOUN DIES (M.) "DAy"

5th Decl	Singular	Plural
Nom	dies	dies
Gen	diei	dierum
Dat	diei	diebus
Acc	diem	dies
Abl	die	diebus

Singular
Nom: dies
Gen: diei
Dat: diei
Acc: diem
Abl: die

Plural
Nom: dies
Gen: dierum
Dat: diebus
Acc: dies
Abl: diebus

NOUNS

DETERMINING THE GENDER AND DECLENSION OF NOUNS

Normally in Latin, nouns ending in -a are feminine and are nouns of the **first declension**. The exceptions are: *agricola* (farmer), *athleta* (athlete), *nauta* (sailor), *poeta* (poet), *pirata* (pirate) and *scriba* (scribe, secretary). These nouns belong to the first declension, but are masculine rather than feminine.

Normally in Latin, nouns ending in –us are masculine, and are nouns of the **second** declension. **The exceptions:** The following nouns are neuter and belong to the third declination: *corpus* (body), *(h)olus* (vegetable), *ius* (right, justice, law, soup), *pectus* (breast), *pondus* (weight) and *tempus* (time). The following nouns are feminine and belong to the fourth declension: *domus* (house), *manus* (hand), and *servitus* (bondage, slavery). The nouns "casus" (case), "fructus" (fruit), "metus" (fear), "senatus" (senate) and "versus" (verse) are masculine, but belong to the fourth declension.

Most nouns ending in -um are neuter and belong to the **second declension**.

For example:

The noun *ampulla* (bottle) is feminine and belongs to the first declension.

The noun *agnus* (lamb) is masculine and belongs to the second declension.

The noun *vinum* (wine) is neuter and belongs to the second declension.

Where I have given two noun forms (the second form is written in italics) and the second form ends in -*is*, these nouns belong to the **third declension** of different sexes. Please see the section on the third declension.

For example:

<u>Masculine</u>
pater, *patris* (father)

<u>Feminine</u>
vox, *vocis* (voice)

<u>Neuter</u>
nomen, *nominis* (name)

Most nouns that end in -*is* are usually feminine and belong to the **third declension**. An exception to this rule is the noun "civis" (citizen), which can be either male or female.

For example:

finis (end)
navis (ship)
turris (tower)

In some cases I will identify the noun using the abbreviations: m. (Masculine), f. (Feminine) and n. (Neuter). I will also identify the declinations with the small numbers 1, 2, 3, 4, and 5.

LATIN/ENGLISH

A-C
Abrilis – April
acetarium, acetaria – salad
acetum – vinegar
actor – actor
adulescens – teen, adolescent
advocatus – lawyer
Aegyptus – Egypt
aestes– summer
ager (m.²) – field, acre
agnus – lamb
agricola (m.) – farmer
allium – garlic
alumna – student, pupil (f.)
alumnus – student, pupil (m.)
amicus – friend (m.)
amor, *amoris* – love
ampulla – bottle
anas, *anatis* – duck
anatina – duck meat (flesh)
Anglice – English
animus – soul, spirit
anno – year
apis – bee
aqua - water
Arabia – Arabia
Arabice - Arabic
aranea – spider
arantium (n.) – orange
arator – farmer, plowman
arbiter – judge

arbor – tree
arena/harena – sand
aries – ram
arquitectus – architect
artifex – architect, artist
Athenae – Athens
athleta (m¹) – athlete
auctor – author
Augustus – August
auris (f.) – ear
autumnus – autumn, fall
avem – bird, fowl

balæna/balena – whale
barba – beard
basium – kiss
brassica – cabbage, cauliflower
bellator – warrior
bellum – war
bos, *bovis* – ox, bull, cow
brachium – arm
Brittania – Great Britain
bubala – beef

caelum – sky
caementarius – mason, stonecutter
Caledonia – Scotland
calix, *calicis* (m³) – glass, cup, goblet
calvaria – skull
cancer, *cancri* (m.²) – crab
canis – dog
cantor – singer, musician
caper, *capri* (m.²) – male goat
capra – female goat

capillus (m.) – hair
caput – leader, head, boss
caput, capitis (n.) – head
carnis – meat, flesh
Carthago – Carthage
caseus – cheese
casus (m.[4]) – case
cathedra – seat, chair
cattus/felis – cat
causa – cause, reason
cena – dinner, supper, meal
cenaculum – upperroom, garret
cervina – venison, game (meat)
cervus – deer
cepa – onion
cerasus – cherry
cerebrum – brain
cervisia – beer
clavis – key
clibanus/fornus – oven
coclear – spoon
cocus – cook
collectarius – banker, cashier
collis –hill
collum – neck
compuntantis – bookkeeper, accountant
coquus – cook
cor, *cordis* (n.) – heart
corpus, *corporis* (n.) – body
corvus – crow, raven
coxa – hip
crocodilus – crocodile
crus, *cruris* (n.) – leg
cubiculum – bedroom, bed

cubitus – bed, sofa
cucumis – cucumber, melon
cucurbita – squash, pumpkin
cucurbitula – zucchini, courgette
culina – kitchen
culpa – guilt
culter – knife

D-H
dactylus – date (fruit)
December – December
dens, *dentis* (m.) – tooth
dies (m.[5]) – day
dies iovis – Thursday
dies lunae – Monday
dies martis – Tuesday
dies mercurii – Wednesday
dies saturni – Saturday
dies solis – Sunday
dies veneris – Friday
digitus – finger
discipula – student, pupil (f.)
discipulus – student, pupil (m.)
dominus – Lord, master
domus (f.[4]) – house, home
donum – gift

elephantus – elephant
equus – horse

faber – smith, carpenter
facies (f.) – face
fama – report, renown, repute

farcimen, *farciminis* – sausage
farina – flour, meal
faux, *faucis, fauces* (f.) – throat, laranyx
Februarius – February
femina – woman
femur (n.) – thigh
fenestra – window
ficus – fig, fig tree
fides (f.[5]) – faith
filia – daughter
filius – son
flumen – river
folium – leaf
forma – form
formica – ant
fortuna – fortune, happiness
frater – brother
frons, *frontis* (f.) – forehead
fructus (m[4]) – fruit
fulgur, fulmen – lightning
furca – fork

Gallia – France
Gallice – French
gallina – hen
gallus – rooster, cockerel
gena – cheek
genu, *genus* (n.) – knee
Germania – Germany
glacies – ice
gloria – glory, fame, honor, renown
grabatus – cot, stretcher, campbed
Graece – Greek
Graecia/Achaea – Greece

grex, *gregis* – herd, flock
gutter, *gutteris* (n.) – throat

Helvatia – Switzterland
herba – grass
Hibernia – Ireland
hiems – winter
Hierosolymum – Jerusalem
Hispania – Spain
Hispanice – Spanish
histrio, *histrionis* – actor
homo, *hominis* – man
holus, *holeris* (n.) – vegetables
hora – hour
hortus – garden
humerus/umerus – shoulder
hydria – jug, pitcher

I-O
iecur, *iecinoris* (n.) – liver
India – India
Indice – Hindi
ira – anger, wrath
Israhel/Iudaea – Israel
Italia – Italy
Italiane – Italian
Iudaice – Hebrew
iudex – judge
ius, *iuris* (n.[3]) – soup, law, right
Ianuarius – January
Iulius – July
Iunius – June

labor, *laboris* – work, labor
labrum – lip
lac, *lactis* – milk
Lacedaemoniis – Sparta
lacerta – lizard
lactuca – lettuce
lacus/mare – lake
lampas, *lampadis* (f.³) – lamp
Latine – Latin
lectulus – sofa, couch
lectus – bed
legumen – legumes, pulse
leo, *leonis* – lion
lepus – rabbit, hare
Libanum – Lebanon
liber, *libri* (m.²) – book
lignarius – carpenter, woodworker
lingua (f.) – tongue, language
Londinium – London
lorica – coat, coat of mail
ludio – player, actor
luna – moon
lupus – wolf

macellarius – butcher
magister – teacher, master (m.)
magistra – teacher, school mistress
Maius – May
malum punicum – pomegranate
malum, pomum – apple
mandíbula/maxilla (f.) – jaw
manus (f.⁴) – hand
mare, *maris* – sea
Martius – March

massa – mass, lump, cake, nugget
mater – mother
medicus – doctor, physician
mel – honey
mens, *mentis* (f.) – mind
mensa – table
mensis – month
mentum – chin
metus (m.[4]) – fear
miles – soldier
militus – soldier
mima, mimula – actress
minister – server, servant, minister
mons, montis – mountain, mount
mora – delay, wait
mors, *mortis* – death
mulier – woman
murus – wall
mus/musculus – mouse, rat
musca – fly
musculus – muscle
musicus – musician

nasus – nose
nauta – sailor, sea man (m.)
navis – ship
Neapoli - Naples
nebula – fog, mist
nimbus – rainstorm, raincloud
nomen, *nominis* – name
nix, *nivis* – snow
nox, *noctis* – night
notarius – notary, secretary
November – November

nubes, *nubis* – cloud
nubila - clouds
nubis – cloud
numerus – number

October– October
oculus – eye
odium – hate
officium – office, function, duty
oleum – oil
oliva – olive
olus, *oleris* (n.) – vegetable
operarius – worker
os, *oris* (n.) – mouth
os, *ossis* (n.) – bone
ostium – door
otium – leisure, freetime
ova – eggs
ovium – sheep
ovum – egg

P-V
pallium – cloak, cape
pane, *panis* – bread
pars, *partis* – part
pascuum – pasture
pastor – shepherd, pastor
patella – plate, dish, saucer
pater, *patris* – father
patria – country, nation
pectus, *pectis* (n.) – chest, breast
pecunia – money
pellis (f.) – skin

periculum – danger
Persice – Persian
persicum – peach, apricot
pes, *pedis* (m.) – foot
philosophia – philosophy
physicus – scientist
pictor – painter
piper, *piperis* – pepper
pirata – pirate
pirum – pear
piscator – fisherman
piscis – fish (m.)
pistor, *pistoris* – baker, miller
pluvia – rain
poena – punishment, penalty, pain
poeta (m.[1]) – poet
pomum, malum – apple
pondus, *ponderis* (n.) – weight
populus – people
porcina – pork
porcus – pig
porta – gate
porticus/vestibulum – porch
praesidens – president
prandium – meal, lunch
pruina/gelu – frost
puella – girl
puer – boy
pullus – chicken
pulmente/pulmentum – soup, stew
pulmo, *pulmonis* (m.) – lung
pupilla – pupil (of the eye)

rana – frog

ratiocinator – bookkeeper, accountant
recubitus – dining room, dining table or couch
ren, renis, renes (m.) – kidney
res (f.[5]) – thing, matter
rex, *regis* – king
Roma - Rome
rosa – rose

sacerdos – priest
sal, *salis* – salt
saliva – saliva, spit, spittle
saltator – dancer
sanguis (m.) – blood
scalae/scalaria/tribunalis – stair(s)
scapula – shoulder (blades), back
schola – school
scriba – scribe, secretary, notary
scriptor – writer
sella – seat, chair
Senatus (m.[4]) – Senate
September – September
septimana – week
sera – lock (of a door, etc.)
serpens – snake, serpent
sessorium – living room
silva – forest, wood(s)
Sina – China
sinapis (f.) – mustard
Sinice – Chinese
sol, *solis* – sun
solarium – balcony
soror – sister
speculum – mirror, looking glass
spes (f.[5]) – hope

spina (f.) – spine
stella – star
sucus – juice

tapete – carpet, rug
taurus/bos – bull
tempestas – weather, storm
templum – temple
tempus (n.) – time
tempus vernum – spring(time)
terra – earth
Theodisce – German
tigris – tiger
tonitrus – thunder
torrens, *torrentis* – stream
trinclinium – dining room
Tunesia – Tunisia
tunica – coat, jacket, shirt
turba – crowd

umbilicus (m.) – navel
umerus/humerus – shoulder
urbs, *urbis* – city
ursus – bear
uva – grape
uva passa – raisin

vacca/bos – cow
Valentia – Valencia
vena – vein, stream
venator – hunter
venter, *ventris* (m.) – stomach
ventus – wind
versus (m.[4]) – verse
vinum – wine

vir – man
vitium – vice, defect
vitulinum – veal
volpes, *volpis* – fox
vox, *vocis* – voice

ENGLISH/LATIN

A-E

accountant – compuntantis, ratiocinator
acre – ager, *agri* (m.²)
actor – actor, histrio, *histrionis*
actor – ludio, *ludionis*
actress – mima, mimula
adolescent – adulescens
anger, wrath – ira
ant – formica
apple – malum, pomum
April – Abrilis
Arabia – Arabia
Arabic – Arabice
architect, artist – arquitectus, artifex
arm – brachium
artist – artifex
Athens – Athenae
athlete – athleta (m.¹)
August – Augustus
author – auctor
autumn/fall – autumnus

back/shoulderblade(s) – scapula
baker – pistor, *pistoris*

balcony – solarium
banker, cashier – collectarius
beans/legumes – legumen (n.)
bear – ursus
beard – barba
bed – lectus
bed/sofa – cubitus
bedroom, bed – cubiculum
bee – apis
beef – bubala(e)
beer – cervisia
bird, fowl – avem
blood – sanguis (m.)
bone – os, *ossis* (n.)
book – liber, *libri* (m.[2])
bookkeeper – compuntantis, ratiocinator
boss, head, leader – caput
bottle – ampulla
boy – puer
brain – cerebrum
bread – pane, *panis*
breast/chest – pectus, *pectis* (n.)
broth/soup – ius, *iuris* (n.[3])
brother – frater
bull, ox – bos, *bovis*, taurus
burden/load – pondus, *ponderis* (n.)
butcher – macellarius

cabbage, cauliflower – brassica
cake/mass – massa
campbed/cot – grabatus
cape/cloak – pallium
carpenter – faber, *fabri*
carpet – tapete

Carthage – Carthago
case – casus (m.⁴)
cat – cattus, felis
cause – causa
chalice – calix, *calicis* (m³)
cheek – gena
cheese – caseus
cherry – cerasus
chicken – pullus
chin – mentum
China – Sina
Chinese – Sinice
city – urbs, *urbis*
cloud – nubes, *nubis*
clouds – nubila
coat – tunica, lorica
coat, coat of mail – lorica
cockerel/rooster – gallus
cook – cocus, coquus
country/nation – patria
courgette/zucchini – cucurbitula
cow – vacca, bos, bovis
crab – cancer, *cancri*
crocodile – crocodilus
crow/raven – corvus
crowd – turba
cucumber/melon – cucumis
cup/chalice – calix, *calicis* (m³)

dancer – saltator
dancer/actor – ludio, *ludionis*
danger – periculum
date (fruit) – dactylus
daughter – filia

day – dies (m.[5])
death – mors, *mortis*
deer – cervus
defect/vice – vitium
delay, wait – mora
dining room, dining sofa – recubitus
dining room – trinclinium
dinner, supper – cena
dinner/meal – cena
dish/saucer – patella
doctor/physician – medicus
dog – canis
door – ostium
duck – anas, *anatis*
duck meat/flesh – anatina
duty/service/vocation – officium

ear – auris (f.)
earth – terra
egg – ovum
eggs – ova
Egypt – Aegyptus
elephant – elephantus
English – Anglice
eye – oculus

F-K

face – facies (f.)
faith – fides (f.[5])
fall/autumn – autumnus
fame/renown – fama
farmer – agricola, arator

farmer, plowman – arator
fatherland, nation – patria
fault, guilt – culpa
fear – metus (m.^{4})
feast – festum
February – Februarius
field – ager, *agri* (m.^{2})
fig – ficus, carica
figtree – ficus
finger – digitus
fish – piscis (m^3)
fisherman – piscator
flesh/meat – carnis
flour – farina
fly – musca
fog – nebula
foot – pes, *pedis* (m.)
forehead – frons, *frontis* (f.)
forest/wood(s) – silva
fork – furca
form – forma
fortune, happiness – fortuna
fox – volpes, *volpis*
France – Gallia
freetime, leisure – otium
French – Gallice
Friday – dies veneris
friend – amicus
frog – rana
frost – pruina, gelu
fruit – fructus (m^4)

garden – hortus
garlic – allium

gate – porta
Germanic Language – Theodisce
Germany – Germania
gift/present – donum
girl – puella
glass, cup, chalice – calix, *calicis* (m^3)
glory, fame, honor – gloria
goat/female goat – capra
goat/male goat – caper, *capri*
goblet/chalice – calix, *calicis* (m^3)
grape – uva
grass – herba
Great Britain – Brittania
Greece – Graecia/Achaea
Greek – Graece
guilt – culpa

hair – capillus
hand – manus (f.[4])
hate – odium
head – caput
heart – cor, cordis
heaven/sky - caelum
Hebrew – Iudaice
hen – gallina
herd, flock – grex, *gregis*
hill – collis
Hindi – Indice
hip – coxa
honey – mel, mellis
hope – spes (f.[5])
horse – equus
house – domus (f.[4])
hunter – venator

ice – glacies
India – India
Ireland – Hibernia
Israel – Israhel/Iudaea
Italian – Italiane
Italy – Italia(m)

January – Ianuarius
jaw – mandíbula/maxilla
Jerusalem – Hierosolymum
Jewish language/Hebrew – Iudaice
judge – arbiter, *arbitri*
judge – iudex
jug/pitcher – hydria
juice – sucus
July – Iulius
June – Iunius
justice/law – ius, *iuris*

key – clavis
kidney – ren, *renis*, renes (m.)
king – rex, *regis*
kiss – basium
kitchen – culina
knee – genu, *genus* (n.)
knife – culter, *cultri*

L-O

lake – lacus, mare
lamb – agnus
lamp – lampas, *lampadis* (f.[3])
language/tongue – lingua

larynx – faux, *faucis*, *fauces* (f.)
Latin – Latine
law – ius, *iuris*
lawyer – advocatus
leader – caput
leaf – folium
Lebanon – Libanum
leg – crus, cruris
legumes/beans – legumen (n.)
leisure, freetime – otium
lettuce – lactuca
lightning – fulgur, fulmen
lion – leo, *leonis*
lip – labrum
liver – iecur, *iecinoris* (n.)
living room – sessorium
lizard – lacerta
load/burden – pondus, *ponderis* (n.)
lock (for a door, etc.) – sera
London – Londinium
lord/Lord – dominus
love – amor, *amoris*
lump, mass, nugget – massa
lunch/meal – prandium
lung – pulmo, *pulmonis* (m.)

mail (armor) – lorica
man – vir, *viri*
March – Martius
mason, stonecutter – caementarius
mass, lump, cake – massa
master/teacher – magister, *magistri*
matter, thing – res (f.[5])
May – Maius

meal (flour) – farina
meal/lunch – prandium
meal/supper – cena
meat/flesh – carnis
melon, cucumber – cucumis
milk – lac, *lactis*
miller, baker – pistor, *pistoris*
mind – mens, *mentis* (f.)
minister, server, servant – minister, *ministri*
mirror – speculum
Monday – dies lunae
money – pecunia
month – mensis
moon – luna
mother – mater, *matris*
mount(ain) – mons, montis
mouse/rat – mus, musculus
mouth – os, *oris* (n.)
muscle – musculus
musician – cantor, musicus
mustard – sinapis (f.)

name – nomen, *nomimis*
Naples – Neapoli
nation – patria
nation, country – patria
navel – umbilicus
neck – collum
nose – nasus
notary – notarius
November – November
nugget, mass, cake – massa
number – numerus

October– October
oil – oleum
olive – oliva
onion – ceba
orange – arantium
oven – clibanus, fornus
ox – bos, *bovis*

P-S

painter – pictor
part – pars, *partis*
pasture – pascuum
peach – persicum
pear – pirum
people – populus
pepper – piper, *piperis*
Persian – Perisce
philosophy – philosophia
physician – medicus
pig – porcus
pirate – pirata (m[1])
pitcher/jug – hydria
plowman/ploughman – arator
poet – poeta (m[1].)
pomegrante – malum punicum
porch – porticus, vestibulum
president – praesidens
priest – sacerdos
pupil (of the eye) – pupilla
pupil/student (f.) – alumna
pupil/student (m.) – alumnus

rabbit, hare – lepus
rain – pluvia
rainstorm, raincloud – nimbus
raisin – uva passa
ram – aries
rat/mouse – mus, musculus
raven/crow – corvus
report/repute/fame – fama
river – flumen
Rome – Roma
rooster/cockerel – gallus
rose – rosa
rumor/renown – fama

sailor – nauta (m.)
salad – acetarium (n.) acetaria (pl.)
salt – sal, *salis*
sand – (h)arena
Saturday – dies saturni
saucer/small plate – patella
sausage – farcimen, farciminis
school – schola
scientist – physicus
Scotland – Caledonia(m)
scribe, secretary – scriba
sea – mare, maris
seat – sella, cathedra
seat, chair – sella, cathedra
secretary, notary – notarius, scriba
Senate – Senatus (m.[4])
September – September
server, servant – minister, *ministri*
service/duty – officium
sheep – ovium

shepherd/pastor – pastor
ship – navis
shouldblade(s)/back – scapula
shoulder – humerus
singer – cantor
sister – soror
skin – pellis (f.)
skull/cranium – calvaria
sky/heaven – caelum
smith, carpenter – faber, *fabri*
snake/serpent – serpens
snow – nix, *nivis*
sofa, couch – lectulus
sofa/bed – cubitus
soldier – miles, *militis*; militus
son – filius
soul/spirit – animus
soup – ius, pulmente, pulmentum
soup/stew – pulmente, pulmentum
Spanish – Hispanice
Sparta – Lacedaemoniis
spider – aranea
spine – spina
spit, spittle, saliva – saliva
spoon – coclear
spring(time) – tempus vernum
squash, pumpkin – cucurbita
stair(s) – scalae, scalaria, tribunalis
star – stella
stomach – venter, *ventris* (m.)
storm – tempestas
storm, weather – tempestas
stream – torrens, *torrentis*
student, pupil (f.) – alumna, discipula

student, pupil (m.) – alumnus, discipulus
summer – aestes
sun – sol, *solis*
Sunday – dies solis
supper/dinner/meal – cena
Switzerland – Helvatia

T-Z

table – mensa
teacher/master – magister, *magistri*
teacher/school mistress – magistra
temple – templum
thigh – femur (n.)
thing, matter – res (f.[5])
throat – faux, *faucis, fauces* (f.)
throat – gutter, *gutteris* (n.)
throat/larynx – faux, *faucis, fauces* (f.)
thunder – tonitrus
Thursday – dies iovis
tiger – tigris
time – tempus, *temporis* (n.)
tongue/language – lingua
tooth – dens, dentis
tree – arbor
Tuesday – dies martis
Tunisia – Tunesia
upperroom, garret – cenaculum
Valencia – Valentia
veal – vitulinum
vegetable – (h)olus, *(h)oleris* (n.)
vein/stream – vena
venison/game – cervina

verse – versus (m.[4])
vice/defect – vitium
vinegar – acetum
voice – vox, *vocis*
wall – murus
war – bellum
warrior - bellator
water – aqua
weather/storm – tempestas
Wednesday – dies mercurii
week – septimana
weight/burden – pondus, *ponderis* (n.)
whale – balæna, balena
wind – ventus
window – fenestra
wine – vinum
winter – hiems
wolf – lupus
woman – mulier, femina
wood(s)/forest – silva
woodworker, carpenter – lignarius
worker – operarius
writer – scriptor

year – anno

zucchini/courgette – cucurbitula

ADIECTIVUM (ADJECTIVES)

Since this book is intended for beginners only, I recommend looking at other sources for more information on adjectives (including comparative and superlative forms). There is also much information on the internet. For example:

https://en.wikipedia.org/wiki/Latin_declension#Adjectives

ADJECTIVES OF THE FIRST AND SECOND DECLENSIONS

novus (new)

SINGULAR

Case	M	F	N
Nom	novus	nova	novum
Gen	novi	novae	novi
Dat	novo	novae	novo
Acc	novum	novam	novum
Abl	novo	nova	novo
Voc	nove	nova	novum

PLURAL

Case	M	F	N
Nom	novi	novae	nova
Gen	novorum	novarum	novorum
Dat	novis	novis	novis
Acc	novos	novas	nova
Abl	novis	novis	novis

| Voc | novi | novae | nova |

The adjectives of the first and second declension have the same forms as their corresponding masculine, feminine, and neutral nouns. They have the same forms, even if the noun they modify has a different form or belongs to a different declension. For example:

magnus (big, great)

With nouns of the *same forms*:

magnus amicus (a great friend)
magna turba (a big crowd)
magnum templum (a great temple)

With nouns of *different forms*:

magnus liber (a great book)
magna mater (a great mother)

ExAMPLE PHRASES

magnus (big, great)

Magnus amicus est.
He is a good friend.
He is a great friend.

Magni amici sunt.
They are good friends.

magna turba
a great crowd
the great (big) crowd

magnae turbae
big crowds

Pirata escribae magnas tunicas dat.
A pirate gives a scribe a big coat.
A pirate gives the scribe the big coat.
The pirate gives the scribe the big coat.

Puellae Piratae magnam tunicam dant.
The girls give the pirate a big coat.

Puellae Piratis magnas tunicas dant.
The girls give the pirates the big coats.
The girls give the pirates some big coats.

multus (much, a lot, many)

Agricola puellae multam pecuniam dat.
A farmer gives a girl a lot of money.
The farmer gives the girl a lot of money.

Puella agricolae multam pecuniam dat.
The girl gives the farmer a lot of money.

bellus (lovely, beautiful, pretty)

Nauta puellae bellam rosam dat.
A sailor gives a girl a pretty rose.
The sailor gives the girl a pretty rose.
The sailor gives the girl the pretty rose.

Please note that most adjectives whose nominative singular form ends in -us belong to the category of the first and second declension (see table). Those adjectives that end in other letters (e.g. "r" like "liber", "x" like "felix" or "s" like "potens") follow different patterns (see tables). Since this book is intended for beginners only, I recommend looking at other sources for more information on adjectives (including comparative and superlative forms). There is also much information on the internet. For example:

https://en.wikipedia.org/wiki/Latin_declension#Adjectives

THE ADJECTIVE NOVUS (NEW)

SINGULAR

Case	M	F	N
Nom	novus	nova	novum
Gen	novi	novae	novi
Dat	novo	novae	novo
Acc	novum	novam	novum
Abl	novo	nova	novo
Voc	nove	nova	novum

PLURAL

Case	M	F	N
Nom	novi	novae	nova
Gen	novorum	novarum	novorum
Dat	novis	novis	novis
Acc	novos	novas	nova
Abl	novis	novis	novis
Voc	novi	novae	nova

THE ADJECTIVE UIBER (FREE)

SINGULAR

Case	M	F	N
Nom	liber	libera	liberum
Gen	liberi	liberae	liberi
Dat	libero	liberae	libero
Acc	liberum	liberam	liberum
Abl	libero	libera	libero
Voc	libere	libera	liberum

PLURAL

Case	M	F	N
Nom	liberi	liberae	libera
Gen	liberorum	liberarum	liberorum
Dat	liberis	liberis	liberis
Acc	liberos	liberas	libera
Abl	liberis	liberis	liberis
Voc	liberi	liberae	libera

THE ADJECTIVE PULCHER (BEAUTIFUL, ATTRACTIVE)

SINGULAR

Case	M	F	N
Nom	pulcher	pulchra	pulchrum
Gen	pulchri	pulchrae	pulchri
Dat	pulchro	pulchrae	puclro
Acc	pulcherum	pulchram	pulchrum
Abl	pulchro	pulchra	pulchro
Voc	pulchre	pulchra	pulchrum

PLURAL

Case	M	F	N
Nom	pulchri	pulchrae	pulchra
Gen	pulchrorum	pulchrarum	pulchrorum
Dat	pulchris	pulchris	pulchris
Acc	pulchros	pulchras	pulchra
Abl	pulchris	pulchris	pulchris
Voc	pulchri	pulchrae	pulchra

ADJECTIVEs LIKE "soLus"

solus (alone, only)

SINGULAR

Case	M	F	N
Nom	solus	sola	solum
Gen	solius	solius	solius
Dat	soli	soli	soli
Acc	solum	solam	solum
Abl	solo	sola	solo
Voc	sole	sola	solum

PLURAL

Case	M	F	N
Nom	soli	solae	sola
Gen	solorum	solarum	solorum
Dat	solis	solis	solis
Acc	solos	solas	sola
Abl	solis	solis	solis
Voc	soli	solae	sola

Here are other adjectives like "solus"

alius – other
alterus – (an)other (between two)
neuter – neither
nullus – none
totus – whole, entire, all
ullus – any
unus – one

uter – either (of two)

THE THIRD DECLENSION

SINGULAR

Case	M	F	N
Nom	Masculine Form	Feminine Form	Neuter Form
Gen	-is	-is	-is
Dat	-i	-i	-i
Acc	-em	-em	Neuter Form
Abl	-i	-i	-i
Voc	Masculine Form	Feminine Form	Neuter Form

PLURAL

Case	M	F	N
Nom	-es	-es	-ia
Gen	-ium	-ium	-ium
Dat	-ibus	-ibus	-ibus
Acc	-es	-es	-ia
Abl	-ibus	-ibus	-ibus
Voc	-es	-es	-ia

For example:

felix (happy)

SINGULAR

Case	M	F	N
Nom	felix	felix	felix
Gen	felicis	felicis	felicis

Dat	felici	felici	felici
Acc	felicem	felicem	felix
Abl	felici	felici	felici
Voc	felix	felix	felix

PLURAL

Case	M	F	N
Nom	felices	felices	felicia
Gen	felicium	felicium	felicium
Dat	felicibus	felicibus	felicibus
Acc	felices	felices	felicia
Abl	felicibus	felicibus	felicibus
Voc	felices	felices	felicia

FELIX AND POTENS

felix (happy)

SINGULAR

Case	M	F	N
Nom	felix	felix	felix
Gen	felicis	felicis	felicis
Dat	felici	felici	felici
Acc	felicem	felicem	felix
Abl	felici	felici	felici
Voc	felix	felix	felix

PLURAL

Case	M	F	N
Nom	felices	felices	felicia

Gen	felicium	felicium	felicium
Dat	felicibus	felicibus	felicibus
Acc	felices	felices	felicia
Abl	felicibus	felicibus	felicibus
Voc	felices	felices	felicia

potens (powerful)

SINGULAR

Case	M	F	N
Nom	potens	potens	potens
Gen	potentis	potentis	potentis
Dat	potenti	potenti	potenti
Acc	potentem	potentem	potens
Abl	potenti	potenti	potenti
Voc	potens	potens	potens

PLURAL

Case	M	F	N
Nom	potentes	potentes	potentia
Gen	potentium	potentium	potentium
Dat	potentibus	potentibus	potentibus
Acc	potentes	potentes	potentia
Abl	potentibus	potentibus	potentibus
Voc	potentes	potentes	potentia

Here are other adjectives of the Third Declension. The second form in italics is the neuter form:

acer/acris, *acre* – fierce
brevis, *breve* – short, brief
crudelis, *crudele* – cruel
fideles, *fidele* – faithful, loyal
gravis, *grave* – serious, severe
omnis, *omne* – all
perennis, *perenne* – perennial, perpetual
regalis, *regale* – regal
recens, *recentis* – recent
sapiens, *sapientis* – wise, rational
similis, *simile* – similar
terribilis, *terribile* – terrible
tristis, *triste* – sad
vetus, *veteris* – old

Please note that adjectives of the third declension may modify nouns of other declensions. In such cases, the forms may be different. For example:

With the Same Form:

turris similis
a similar tower
the similar tower

With Different Forms:

murus similis
a similar wall

causa similis
a similar cause

donum similis
a similar gift

ADJECTIVES (ALPHABETICAL LIST)

LATIN/ENGLISH

Since this book is intended for beginners only, I recommend looking at other sources for more information on adjectives (including comparative and superlative forms). There is also much information on the internet. For example:

https://en.wikipedia.org/wiki/Latin_declension#Adjectives

acerbus – bitter, acrid, severe
albus – white
alius, alterus – (an)other
altus – tall, high
amicus – nice, friendly
antiqus – old
anxius, sollicitus – worried
arantius – orange
attentus – careful, attentive
aureus – golden

beatus – happy, fortunate, blessed
bellus – pretty, handsome, charming
bonus – good
brevis – short, small, brief
brun(i)us– brown
brunus, brunetus – brown-haired

caerul(e)us/azureus – blue
carus – dear
celer – swift, quick, rapid
certus – definite, sure

clarus – clear, bright, renowned, famous
comis, urbanus – polite
contentus – content, satisfied
crassus – fat
crudelis, *crudele* – cruel

deformis, turpis – ugly
depressus – depressed
difficilis – difficult
dilligens – diligent, hardworking
dulcis – sweet
durus – hard
facilis – easy, simple
felix – happy
festivus – fun, enjoyable
fidelis – faithful, loyal
flavus – yellow, blond
fortis – strong, brave

gravis – heavy, serious, grave, grievous
griseus – gray, grey

humanus – human

immortalis – immortal
industrius, sedulus – industrious, hardworking
infirmus, malus – ill, sick
iniudundus – unpleasant
intellegens – intelligent
iocosus/comicus - funny
iratus – angry
iucundus – pleasant, interesting

lassus/defussus – tired

liber, *libera, liberum* – free
longus – long

magnus – great
malus – bad
medius – middle
miser – wretched, miserable, unfortunate
mortuus – dead
multus, multi – much, many

nervosus, trepidus, timidis – nervous
niger, *nigra, nigrum* – black
novus – new
novus, iucundus – interesting
nullus – none

odiosis, molestus, longinquus – boring
omnis – all, every
optimus – best
otiosus, tiger, iners – lazy, inactive

parvus – small, little
perennis, *perenne* – perpetual
placidus – calm, tranquil
pontens – powerful, strong, able
primus – first, best
pulcher, *pulchra, pulchrum* – beautiful
purpura – purple
pusillanimis – discouraged

regalis, *regale* – regal, royal
recens, *recentis* – recent
Romanus – Roman
roseus – pink
ruber – red

rubicundus – red, reddish
rudis – rude, impolite
rufus – red, red-haired, ruddy

sapiens, *sapientis* – wise
senex – old, aged
serius, gravis – serious, grave
similis, *simile* – similar
sollicitus – worried, busy
solus – alone, only
studiosus – eager, industrious
stultus – foolish, stupid
sufflavus, subflavus, flavus – blond

tenius – thin
terribilis, *terribile* – terrible
totus – whole, entire
trepidus/pavidus – afraid
tristis – sad
turbatus – irritated
turpis – shameful, base, disgraceful

ultimus – last
unus – one

veridis – green
verus – true
vetus, *veteris* – old

ENGLISH/LATIN

Since this book is intended for beginners only, I recommend looking at other sources for more information on adjectives (including comparative and superlative forms). There is also much information on the internet. For example:

https://en.wikipedia.org/wiki/Latin_declension#Adjectives

afraid – trepidus, pavidus
all, every – omnis
alone, only – solus
angry – iratus
attractive, cute, pretty, handsome – bellus
average, mean – medius

bad – malus
beautiful, pretty, lovely – bellus, pulcher
best – optimus, primus
big, large, great – magnus
bitter, harsh, severe – acerbus
black – niger, *nigra*, *nigrus*
blond – flavus, sufflavus, subflavus
blue – caerulus, caeruleus, azureus
boring – odiosis, molestus, longinquus
brave, strong – fortis
brief, short – brevis
brown – brunus, brunius
brown-haired – brunus, brunetus

calm, tranquil – placidus
clear – clarus
comical, funny – comicus, iocosus
continual, perpetual – perennis, *perenne*

cruel – crudelis, *crudele*

dead – mortus
dear – carus
depressed – depressus
discouraged – pusillanimis

easy, simple – facilis
elderly, old – senex
enjoyable, fun – festivus
entire, whole – totus
eternal – immortalis
every, all – omnis
expensive – carus, pretiosus

faithful, loyal – fidelis
famous, renowned – clarus, nomitnaus
fast – celer, velox
fat – crassus
first – primus
foolish, stupid – stultus
free – liber, libera, liberum
fun – festivus
fun, enjoyable – festivus

glorious, illustrious – illustris, clarus
golden – aureus
good – bonus
gray/grey – griseus
great, big, large – magnus
green – viridis

handsome, attractive – bellus
happy – felix, beatus
hard – durus
hard, difficult – dificilis, acerbus

hardworking – sedulus, industrius, studiosus
harsh, bitter, severe – acerbus
high – altus
human – humanus

idle, lazy – otiosus, tiger, iners
ill, sick – infirmus, malus
immortal, eternal – immortalis
impolite, rude – rudis
important – clarus, magnus, sonticus, propensus
intelligent – intellegens
interesting – iucundus, novus
irritated – turbatus, iratus

last – ultimus
lazy – otiosus, tiger, iners
little, small, brief – parvus, brevis
long – longus

mindful, heedful, observant – erectus, memor, attentus, dilligens
much, many – multus, multum, multi

nervous – nervosus, trepidus, timidis
new, strange – novus
nice, friendly – amicus, gratus, iucundus
none – nullus

old – antiquis, senex, vetus
only, alone – solus
orange – arantius
other, another – alius, alterus

perpetual – perennis, *perenne*
pink – roseus
pleasant, interesting – iucundus
polite, urbane – comis, urbanus

powerful, strong – pontens
purple – purpura

recent – recens, *recentis*
reddish – rubicundus, rufus
red-haired – ruber, rubicundus, rufus
regal, royal – regalis, regale
Roman – Romanus
rude, impolite – rudis

sad – tristis
satisfied, content – contentus
serious – serius, gravis
serious, grave – serius, gravis
short, brief – brevis
similar – similis, *simile*
simple – facilis
small, little, brief – parvus, brevis
strange – novus
strong – fortis, pontens
stupid, foolish – stultus
sure – certus
sweet – dulcis

tall – altus
terrible – terribilis, *terribile*
thin – tenius
tired – lassus, defussus
true – verus

ugly – deformis, turpis
unpleasant – iniucundus

white – albus
whole, entire – totus

wise – sapiens
worried – anxius, sollicitus
wretched, pitiful – miser

yellow – flavus

VERB FORMS IN LATIN

Most verbs in the Latin language have six verb forms (in the indicative *). In this book, they are presented in the following order:

Singular
1. **ego** (I)
2. **tu** (you)
3. **is/ea/id** (he/she/it)

Plural
4. **nos** (we)
5. **vos** (you all)
6. **ei/eae/ea** (they)

For example:

The Verb *esse* (to be):

sum
es
est
sumus
estis
sunt

That is to say:

ego **sum** (I *am*)
tu **es** (you *are*)
is/ea/id **est** (he/she/it *is*)

nos **sumus** (we *are*)
vos **estis** (you *are*)

ei/eae/ea **sunt** (they *are*)

*Since this is a book for beginners, we will not cover the topics of other verbal modes (e.g. imperative, conjunctive, passive, etc.).

Please note:

Latin verbs are generally called (named) by their first person singular form in the present indicative tense (rather than the infinitive form). For example:

habeo – I have (first person singular)
habere – to have (infinitive form)

In this book, I will use both ways of calling verbs.

THE –ARE VERBS

THE FIRST CONJUGATION

THE VERB AMO/AMARE (TO LOVE)

ego am**o** – I love
tu am**as** – you love
is/ea am**at** – he/she/it loves

nos am**amus** – we love
vos am**atis** – you all love
ei/eae am**ant** – they love

OTHER VERBS OF THE FIRST CONJUGATION

The following verbs are conjugated like the verb *amare*:

ambulare – to walk
auscultare – to listen
cogitare – to think
dare – to give
habitare – to live, reside
iuvare – to help
lavare – to wash
laborare – to work
manducare – to eat
necare – to kill
saltare – to dance
vocare – to call, name
volare – to fly

ExAMPLE SENTENCES

Poeta amat me.
Poeta me amat.
Me amat Poeta.
A poet loves me.
The poet loves me.

Poeta non me amat.
The poet doesn't love me.

Poetam amo.
I love a poet.
I love the poet.

Amas me.
Me amas.
Tu me amas.
You love me.

Non me amas.
You don't love me.

Filiam nostram amamus.
We love our daughter.

Filiae nostrae nos amat.
Our daughter loves us.

Amant filium eorum.
Filium eorum amant.
They love their son.

Agricola puellae multam pecuniam dat.
A farmer gives a girl a lot of money.
The farmer gives the girl a lot of money.

Puella agricolae multam pecuniam dat.
The girl gives the farmer a lot of money.

Nauta puellae bellam rosam dat.
A sailor give a girl a pretty rose.
The sailor gives the girl a pretty rose.
The sailor gives the girl the pretty rose.

Pirata escribae magnas tunicas dat.
A pirate gives a scribe a big coat.
A pirate gives the scribe the big coat.
The pirate gives the scribe the big coat.

Puellae Piratae magnam tunicam dant.
The girls give the pirate a big coat.

Puellae Piratis magnas tunicas dant.
The girls give the pirates the big coats.
The girls give the pirates some big coats.

THE –ERE VERBS

THE SECOND CONJUGATION

THE VERB VIDEO/VIDERE (TO SEE)

ego vid**eo** – I see
tu vid**es** – you see
is/ea vid**et** – he/she sees

nos vid**emus** – we see
vos vid**etis** – you all see
ei/eae vid**ent** – they see

OTHER VERBS OF THE SECOND CONJUGATION

Here are some other verbs like the verb *videre*:

ardere – to burn
debere – to owe, ought, shall
docere – to teach
flere – to cry
iubere – to order
manere – to wait
miscere – to mix
monere – to warn, advise
movere – to move
parere – to appear, obey, fulfill*
pendere – to hang
respondere – to respond, answer
ridere – to laugh

sedere – to sit
tenere – to hold
terrere – to frighten
timere – to fear

* not to be confused with parere (pario) of the third conjugation (see -io verbs), which means to bear children, beget or produce.

ExAMPLE SENTENCES

Amicum meum in foro video.
I see my friend at the market.

Filium nostrum in agro videmus.
We see our son in the field.

Multum magister docet me.
Magister multum docet me.
Magister multum me docet.
The teacher teaches me a lot.

Quid debemus cogitare?
What should we think?

Nihil te terret.
Nothing frightens you.

Omnia timeo.
I fear everything.

THE THIRD CONJUGATION

THE VERB BIBO/BIBERE (TO DRINK)

ego bib**o** – I drink
tu bib**is** – you drink
is/ea bib**it** – he/she drinks

nos bib**imus** – we drink
vos bib**itis** – you all drink
ei/eae bib**unt** – they drink

OTHER VERBS OF THE THIRD CONJUGATION

carpere – to pick, seize*
dicere – to say
ducere – to lead
currere – to run
legere – to read
scribere – to write
vivere – to live

Carpe diem! (Seize the day!)

The following verbs have an irregular stem in the Perfect Tense:

dicere (dix-)
ducere (dux-)
currere (cucurr-)
scribere (scrips-)
vivere (vix-)

Please see the Verb Tables.

THE VERB DICO/DICERE (TO SAY)

ego dic**o** – I say
tu dic**is** – you say
is/ea dic**it** – he/she says

nos dic**imus** – we say
vos dic**itis** – you all say
ei/eae dic**unt** – they say

Ego autem dico vobis quia omnis qui irascitur fratri suo reus erit iudicio.

But I say to you all, whoever becomes angry with his brother will be found guilty.

-*Vulgate*, Matt. 5:22

Facto vespere dicitis: "Serenum erit rubicundum est enim caelum". Et mane dicitis: "Hodie tempestas rutilat enim triste caelum".

When evening comes, you say, "It will be nice weather, because the sky is red".And in the morning you say, "Today there will be a storm, because the sky is red and threatening." -*Vulgate*, Matt. 16:3

Venit enim Iohannes neque manducans neque bibens et dicunt daemonium habet.

John came neither eating and drinking and they say "He has a demon".
– *Vulgate*, Matt. 11:18

THE -IO VERBS LIKE FACERE

There is a group of verbs called the "-io verbs" because the first form ends with -io. For example, here is the verb *facere*:

facio/facere (to do, make)

ego fac**io**
tu fac**is**
is/ea fac**it**

nos fac**imus**
vos fac**itis**
ei/eae fac**iunt**

Here are other verbs like *facere*:

accipere – to take, receive
capere – to take, catch
fodere – to dig
fugere – to flee
iacere – to throw
parere – to bear, beget, produce*
rapere – to grab, snatch, carry off

*not to be confused with *parere* (pareo) of the 2nd conjugation which means to appear, obey, fulfill or comply.

THE –IRE VERBS

THE FOURTH CONJUGATION

THE VERB AUDIO/AUDIRE (TO HEAR)

ego audi**o** – I hear
tu aud**is** – you hear
is/ea aud**it** – he/she hears

nos aud**imos** – we hear
vos aud**itis** – you all hear
ei/eae aud**iunt** – they hear

Dixitque Samuhel et: Quae est haec vox gregum quae resonat in auribus meis et armentorum quam ego audio?

And Samuel said, "What is this bleating (voice) of sheep in my ears and this animal noise that I hear?"

Vulgate, Samuel 15: 14

OTHER VERBS OF THE FOURTH CONJUGATION

aperire (to open)
pervenire (to arrive, reach)
sentire (to feel)
venire (to come)

IRREGULAR VERBS

Please see the Verb Tables at the end of this book.

ESSE (TO BE)

Present	Imperfect	Perfect	Future
sum	eram	fui	ero
es	eras	fuisti	eris
est	erat	fuit	erit
sumus	eramus	fuimus	erimus
estis	eratis	fuistis	eritis
sunt	erant	fuerunt	erunt

IN THE PRESENT

sum
es
est
sumus
estis
sunt

IN THE IMPERFECT PAST

eram
eras
erat

eramus
eratis
erant

IN THE PERFECT PAST

fui
fuisti
fuit
fuimus
fuistis
fuerunt

IN THE FUTURE

ero
eris
erit
erimus
eritis
erunt

IRE (TO GO)

Present	Imperfect	Perfect	Future
eo	ibam	ii	ibo
is	ibas	iste	ibis
is	ibat	iit	ibit
imus	ibamus	iimus	ibimus
itis	ibatis	istis	ibitis
eunt	ibant	ierunt	ibunt

POSSE (CAN, TO BE ABLE)

Present	Imperfect	Perfect	Future
possum	poteram	potui	potero
potes	poteras	potuisti	poteris
potest	poterat	potuit	poterit
possumus	poteramus	potuimus	poterimus
potestis	poteratis	potuistis	poteritis
possunt	poterant	potuerunt	poterunt

Please see the Verb Tables at the end of this book.

MALLE (TO PREFER)

Present	Imperfect	Perfect	Future
malo	malebam	malui	malam
mavis	malebas	maluisti	males
mavult	malebat	maluit	malet
malumus	malebamus	maluimus	malemus
mavultis	malebatis	maluistis	maletis
malunt	malebant	maluerunt	malent

VELLE (TO WANT, WISH)

Present	Imperfect	Perfect	Future
volo	volebam	volui	volam
vis	volebas	voluisti	voles
vult	volebat	voluit	volet
volumus	volebamus	voluimus	volemus
vultis	volebatis	voluistis	voletis
volunt	volebant	voluerunt	volent

NOLLE (TO NOT WANT, WISH)

Present	Imperfect	Perfect	Future
nolo	nolebam	nolui	nolam
non vis	nolebas	noluisti	noles
non vult	nolebat	noluit	nolet
nolumus	nolebamus	noluimus	nolemus
non vultis	nolebatis	noluistis	noletis
nolunt	nolebant	noluerunt	nolent

THE VERB *LOQUOR* (TO SPEAK, TALK)

Present
- loquor
- loqueris
- loquitur
- loquimur
- loquimi
- loquuntur

Future
- loquar
- loqueris
- loquetur
- loquemur
- loquemini
- loquentur

Imperfect
- loquebar
- loquebaris
- loquebatur
- loquebamur
- loquebamini
- loquebantur

Perfect
- locutus sum
- locutus es

| locutus est |
| locuti sumus |
| locuti estis |
| locuti sun |

The verb "loquor" is an example of what is known as a "deponent" verb. Such verbs use verb forms which are like the normal "passive" verb forms. Please remember, that such verb moods such as the conditional, passive and imperative will not be dealt with in this book, as it is intended for beginners.

VERBS (ALPHABETICAL LIST)

LATIN/ENGLISH

accipere – receive, take
adiuvare/iuvare – help
agere – drive, lead, do act
amare – love
ambulare – walk
aperire – open
ardere – burn
audere – dare
audire – hear, listen
auscultare – listen

bibere – drink

canere, cantare – sing
capere – take
carere – want, lack, be deprived of, be free from
carpere – pick, pluck, seize
cogitare – think, consider, plan
comedere – eat
committere – commit, entrust
conservare – keep, save, conserve
continere – hold together, contain, keep, enclose, restrain
creare – create
credere – believe, trust
currere – run

dare – give
debere – owe, ought, must
delere – destroy, wipe out, erase

delineare – draw, sketch
deportare – carry away
dicere – say, tell
docere – teach
ducere – lead

egere – have need of, be in need
equitare – ride horseback
errare – to err, wander, go astray
esse – be
exercere – exercise, train
expellere – drive out, expel

facere – do, make
flere – cry
fodere – dig
fugere – flee

gerere – carry, carry on, manage, conduct, accomplish

habere – have, hold, possess
habitare – live, stay, reside

iacere – throw, hurl
incipere – begin
ire, vadere – go
iubere – order
iuvare – help

laborare – work
lavare – wash
laudare – praise
legere – read, choose, elect
liberare – free, liberate
loquor – speak, talk
ludere – play

malle – prefer
manducare – eat
manere – remain, stay, wait
miscere – mix
monere – advise, warn
movere – move, arouse, affect
mutare – change, alter, exchange

narrare – tell, report, narrate
natare – swim
necare – kill
negare – deny, say that...not
neglegere – neglect, disregard
nolle – not want, not wish
nuntiare – announce, report, relate

opprimere – suppress, overwhelm, overpower, check

parare – prepare, provide, get, obtain
parere (pareo) – appear, comply, obey, fulfill (2nd conjugation)
parere – bear, beget, produce (3rd conj.)
pellere – strike, push, drive out
pendere – hang
pervenire – arrive, reach
petere – seek, aim at, beg, beseech
pingere – paint
posse – can, be able
postulare – need, request
premere – press, press hard
putare – reckon, suppose, judge

quaerere – ask, enquire, look for

rapere – sieze, snatch, carry away
recusare – refuse, reject

relinquere – leave behind, abandon
remanere – remain, stay, abide, continue
respondere – respond, answer
ridere – laugh
rogare – ask, seek

saltare – dance
salvere – be in good health
scribere – write
sedere – sit
sentire – feel
servare – keep, save
sperare – hope for
stare – stand
studere – be eager, to study
superare – be above, surpass, overcome, conquer

tangere – touch
tenere – have, hold, keep, possess
terrere – frighten, terrify
timere – fear, be afraid of
tollere – raise, lift up, take away, remove, destroy
trahere – draw, drag

vadere, ire – go
valere – be strong, well, have power
velle – want, wish
venire – come
videre – see, understand
vincere – conquer, overcome
vitare – avoid
vivere – live
vocare – call, summon
volare – fly
volere – wish, be willing, will

ENGLISH/LATIN

act, do, drive, lead – agere
advise, warn – monere
answer – respondere
appear, be evident – parere
arrive, reach – pervenire
ask, enquire, ask about – quaerere
ask for, look for – quaerere

be – esse
burn – ardere

call, summon – vocare
can, be able – posse
come – venire
comply, obey, fulfill – parere
cry, weep – flere

dance – saltare
dig – fodere
do, make – facere
draw, sketch – delineare
drink – bibere

eat – comedere, manducare
enquire, ask about – quaerere
exercise – exercere

fear – timere
feel – sentire
flee – fugere
fly – volare
frighten – terrere

give – dare
go – ire, vadere

hang – pendere
have – habere
hear, listen – audire
help – iuvare
hold – tenere

kill – necare

laugh – ridere
lead – ducere
like, love – amare
listen, hear – auscultare
live – vivere
live, reside – habitare
love, like – amare

make, do – facere
mix – miscere
move – movere

need – postulare
not want – nolle

obey, fulfill – parere
open – aperire
order – iubere
owe, ought, should – debere

paint – pingere
pick, pluck, seize – carpere
play – ludere
prefer – malle

read – legere

receive, take – accipere
remain, stay, wait – manere
ride horseback – equitare
run – currere

say, tell – dicere
see – videre
seize, catch, carry off – rapere
sing – canere, cantare
sit – sedere
stand – stare
stay, remain, wait – manere
speak, talk – loquor
swim – natare

take, catch – capere
take, receive – accipere
talk, speak – loquor
teach – docere
think – cogitare
throw – iacere
train, exercise – exercere

wait, remain, stay – manere
walk – ambulare
want, wish – velle
not want – nolle
warn – monere
wash – lavare
work – laborare
write – scribere

MISCELLANEOUS VERBS AND PHRASES

<u>-are verbs</u>
adiuvare/iuvare – help
amare – love
cogitare – think, consider, ponder, plan
conservare – keep, save, conserve
creare – create
dare – give
deportare – carry away
errare – to err, wander, go astray
laudare – praise
liberare – free, liberate
manducare – eat
mutare – change, alter, exchange
narro – tell, report, narrate
negare – deny, say that...not
nuntiare – announce, report, relate
parare – prepare, provide, get, obtain
putare – reckon, suppose, judge
recusare – refuse, reject
rogare – ask, seek
servare – keep, save
sperare – hope for
superare – be above, surpass, overcome, conquer
vitare – avoid
vocare – call, summon
volare – fly

<u>-ere verbs</u>
agere – drive, lead, do act
audere – dare
bibere – drink

carere – want, lack, be deprived of, be free from
committere – commit, entrust
continere – hold together, contain, keep, enclose, restrain
credere – believe, trust
currere – run
debere – owe, ought, must
delere – destroy, wipe out, erase
docere – teach
ducere – lead, consider, regard
egere – have need of, be in need
expellere – drive out, expel
facere – do, make
gerere – carry, carry on, manage, conduct, accomplish
iacere – throw, hurl
incipere – begin
legere – choose, elect, read
habere – have, hold, possess
monere – advise, warn
movere – move, arouse, affect
neglegere – neglect, disregard
opprimere – suppress, overwhelm, overpower, check
pellere – strike, push, drive out
petere – seek, aim at, beg, beseech
premere – press, press hard
quaerere – ask, ask for, enquire (about)
remanere – remain, stay, abide, continue
rapere – sieze, snatch, carry away
relinquere – leave behind, abandon
ridere – laugh
salvere – be in good health
scribere - write
studere – be eager, to study
tangere – touch
tenere – have, hold, keep, possess

terrere – frighten, terrify
timere – fear, be afraid of
tollere – raise, lift up, take away, remove, destroy
trahere – draw, drag
valere – be strong, well, have power
videre – see, understand
vincere – conquer, overcome
volere – wish, be willing, will

volo – I want (to), I am willing

dico – I say
tibi dico – I say to you (singular)
vobis dico – I say to you all (plural)

-ire verbs
scire – know

present simple
ait – he says
ait illi – he says to him/her
ait illis – he says to them
exsurgens – rising up, getting up, standing up
dicit – he says
facit – he makes
surdos facit audire et mutos loqui – he makes the deaf hear and the dumb speak
oboediunt – they obey
oboediunt ei – they obey him
oporteat – he should, he must
oporteat venire primum – he must come first
quaerit – he seeks, looks for
querunt – they seek, look for
quaerunt te – they are looking for you, they are asking for you

gerunds
ascendens – going up (into), getting into (e.g. a boat)
circumspiciens – looking around
dicens – saying
dormiens – sleeping
respondens eis – answering them
stans – being, standing

perfect and imperfect past
ait – he said (also he says)
ait illi – he said to him/her
ait illis – he said to them
apparuit – he appeared, there appeared
apparuit illis – there appeared to them (Elijah)
benedixit – he blessed
ipsos benedixit – he blessed them (the fishes)
coepit – he began
coepit docere – he began to teach
dabat – he gave, was giving
dedit – he gave
dedit eis – he gave to them
dicebat – he said, he was saying
dimisit – he dimissed, sent away
dimisit eos – he sent them away
dixit – he said
dixerunt – they said
docebat – he taught, he was teaching
donavit – he gave, has given
edebat – he ate, he was eating
erat – he was
erant – they were
exclamavit – he exclaimed, cried out
exiit – he went out, has gone out
extendit – he extended, stretch out

extendit manum suam – he stretched out his hand
fecit – he did, has done
bene omnia fecit – he has done all things well
fregi – I broke
fregit – he broke
ibant – they went, they would go
intravit – he entered
interrogavit – he asked
interrogavit eos – he asked them
manducaret – he ate, was eating
manducaverunt – they ate
misit – he put
petiit – he asked for, begged for
poterat – he wanted, desired
praecepit – he commanded
praecepit illis – he commanded them
procidit – he fell down, collapsed
respondit – he responded, answered
responderunt – they answered
responderunt ei – they answered him
timebant – they feared, they were afraid
vidimus – we saw
volebat – he wanted, was wanting

Commands
audite – Hear!/Listen! (plural)
Audite illum! – Hear him!/Listen to him!
extende manum tuam – Stretch your hand!
Ite and vedite! – Go and see! (plural)
Pete a me quod vis et dabo tibi. – Ask me whatever you want, and I'll give it to you.
surge – Stand up!
tace! – be still!, be quiet!
vade – Go!

Ite in civitatem! – Go ye to the city!
Vade retro me, Satana! – Get behind me, Satan!
Vale in domum tuam! – Go home!/Go to your house!

miscellaneous
bene facere – to do good
male facere – to do evil

veni – I came
venit – he came
venisti – you came
vidit – he saw
vocavit – he called

dicit eis – he says to them
dicit homini – he says to the man

dicebat – he said, he was saying

docebat eos – he taught them
fecit – he made
introivit – he entered
sedebat circa eum turba – a crowd sat (was sitting) around him
vocavit illos – he called them

dicebant – they said, they were saying
dixerent ei – they said to him
(illi) tacebant – they were silent, said nothing, held their peace
observabant eum – they watched him
secuti sunt eum – they followed him
venerunt ad eum – they came to him
quidam enim ex eis de longe venerunt – for some of them have come from afar
veniunt ad domum – they came (having come?) to a house

Omnes quaerunt te – Everyone's looking for you/Everyone's asking about you

THE VERB *HABERE* (HAVE)

The Verb *habeo* (habere)

ego **habeo** – I have
tu **habes** – you have
is **habet** – he has
ea **habet** – she has
id **habet** – it has

nos **habemus** – we have
vos **habetis** – you all have
ei **habent** – they have (m.)
eae **habent** – they have (f.)
ea **habent** – they have (n.)

Librum habeo.
I have a book./I have the book.

Librum non habeo.
I have no book.
I don't have a book.
I don't have the book.

THE VERB *POSTULARE* (TO NEED)

postulare (to need, request)

ego **postulo** – I need
tu **postulas** – you need
is **postula** – he needs
ea **postula** – she needs
id **postula** – it needs

nos **postulamus** – we need
vos **postulatis** – you all need
ei/eae/ea **postulant** – they need

Librum postulo.
I need a book.
I need the book.

Librum non postulo.
I don't need a book.
I don't need the book.

chartam, papyrum – paper
libellum – a notebook, pamphlet
librum – a book
mensam – a table, desk
stilum – a pen, stylus
tabellam/tabulam – a writing tablet, board

AD LUDUM (IN CLASS)

ad ludum
(at school, in the classroom)

HABEO... (I HAVE...)

ego **habeo** – I have
tu **habes** – you have
is **habet** – he has
ea **habet** – she has
id **habet** – it has

nos **habemus** – we have
vos **habetis** – you all have
ei **habent** – they have (m.)
eae **habent** – they have (f.)
ea **habent** – they have (n.)

Librum habeo.
I have a book./I have the book.

Librum non habeo.
I have no book.
I don't have a book.
I don't have the book.

auxilium – help, aid
chartam, papyrum – paper
libellum – a notebook
librum – a book
mensam – a desk, table
sellam – a chair

stilum – a pen, stylus
tabellam/tabulam – a writing tablet

POSTULO... (I NEED...)

ego **postulo** – I need
tu **postulas** – you need
is **postula** – he needs
ea **postula** – she needs
id **postula** – it needs

nos **postulamus** – we need
vos **postulatis** – you all need
ei/eae/ea **postulant** – they need

Librum postulo.
I need a book.
I need the book.

Librum non postulo.
I don't need a book.
I don't need the book.

auxilium – help
chartam, papyrum – paper
libellum – a notebook, pamphlet
librum – a book
mensam – a table, desk
sellam – a chair
stilum – a pen, stylus
tabellam/tabulam – a writing tablet, board

EST... (THERE IS...)

charta – paper
libellus – a notebook
liber – a book
mensa – a desk, table
sella – a chair
stilus – a pen, stylus
tabella/tabula – a writing tablet

HOMINES (PEOPLE)

magister – the teacher, master
magistra – the teacher, mistress

alumnus/discipulus – the student, pupil
alumna/discipula – the student, pupil (f.)

puer – the boy
pueri – the boys

puella – the girl
puellae – the girls

vir – the man
viri – the men

mulier – the woman
mulieres – the women

adulescuns/iuventus – the teen (m.)
iuventa – the teen (young lady)

domine – the lord, gentleman
domina – the mistress, lady

SALUTEM (GREETINGS AND FAREWELLS)

Salve!/Ave! – Hello! (Singular)
Salvete!/Avete! Hello! (Plural)

Vales?
Ut vales?
Quomodo vales?
How are you?

Valetis?
Ut valetis?
Quo modo valetis?
How are you all?

Valeo... – I am...
Valemus... – We are...

bene – good, fine, well
male – bad, not well
non bene – not well, not good

Bene valeo. – I'm fine.
Male valeo. – I'm not well.

Bene valemus. – We're fine.
Male valemus. – We're not well.

Bene, et tu?
Fine, and you?

Bene, et vos?
Fine, and you all?

Vale!

Good-bye!/Farewell! (Singular)

Valete!
Good-bye! (Plural)

Cura ut valeas – Take care!

VERBA UTILIA (USEFUL WORDS AND PHRASES)

domine – sir, mister
domina – madam, ma'am, Mrs.

etiam/sic (est)/vero (est) - yes
non – no
fortasse – maybe, perhaps

Obsecro./Quaeso. – Please.

Gratias. – Thanks.

Gratias tibi.
I thank you.

magnas gratias, magnas gratias ago
Thanks you very much.
Many thanks.

maximas gratias, maximas gratias ago, ingentes gratias ago
Thank you so much.
Thanks a million.

Libenter.
You're welcome. (Gladly)

Salve!/Salavete! – Welcome!

Gratulationes! – Congratulations!

Sanitas!/Et sanitas tua! – Cheers!

Ego tibi! – At your service!

Te adiuvare possum?
Can I help you?

Quaeso mihi permittere?
May I?

Certe!/Scilicet!
Of course!

Paenitet (me).
I am sorry.

Intellego.
I understand.

Non intellego.
I don't understand.

Precor ut loquaris lente.
Please, speak more slowly.

FAM L A (THE FAM LY)

Hic maritus meus est.
This is my husband.

Haec uxor mea est.
This is my wife.

Haec sponsa mea est.
This is my bride.
This is my fiancée.

Hic est filius meus.
This is my son.

Haec filia mea est.
This is my daughter.

Hi sunt filii mei.
These are my sons.

Hae sunt filiae meae.
These are my daughters.

Hi sunt liberos meos.
These are my children.

pater – father
mater – mother

parentes – parents
cognati – relatives

avus – grandfather
avia – grandmother

nepos – grandson
neptis – granddaughter

frater – brother
soros – sister

frates – brothers
sororibus – sisters

consobrinus/patruelis – cousin (m.)
consobrina/patruelis – cousin (f.)

avunculus/patruus – uncle
amita/matertera – aunt

fratis filius/sororis filius – nephew
fratis filia/sororis filia – niece

amicus – friend (m.)
amica– friend (f.)

optimus amicus – best friend (m.)
optima amica – best friend (f.)

comes/socius – good friend, comrade

OFFICIIS (TRADES AND PROFESSIONS)

THE VERB *ESSE* (*TO BE*)

esse (to be)

ego **sum**... – I am...

tu **es**... – you are...

is **est**... – he is...
ea **est**... – she is...
id **est**... – it is...

nos **sumus**... – we are...

vos **estis**... – you all are...

ei **sunt**... – they are... (m.)
eae **sunt**... – they are... (f.)
ea **sunt**... – they are... (n.)

Puer sum. – I am a boy.
Puella sum. – I am a girl.

Vir est. – He is a man.
Mulier est. – She is a woman.

Discipulus sum. – I am a student.
Medicus sum. – I am a doctor/physician.

Magistra est. – She is a teacher.

THE VERBS *AGERE* AND *FACERE*

AGERE (ACT, DO)
ago, agere (act, do)

ego **ago** – I *do*
tu **agis** – you *do*
is/ea **agit** – he/she *does*

nos **agimus** – we *do*
vos **agitis** – you all *do*
ei/eae **agunt** – they *do*

Quid agis in opus tuum?
What do you do in your job?

Quid agis?
What do you do?

FACERE (DO, MAKE)

ego **facio** – I do
tu **facis** – you do
is/ea **facit** – he/she does

nos **facimus** – we do
vos **facitis** – you all do
ei/eae **faciunt** – they do

Quid facitis?
What do you all do?

WHAT DO YOU DO FOR A LIVING?

Quod est officium tuum?
What is your profession?

Quid agis in opus tuum?
What do you do in your job?
What do you do at work?

Advocatus sum.
I'm a lawyer.

Ubi laboras?
Where do you work?

Laboro in officium.
I work in an office.
I work work in a factory.

...sum – I am a(n)...

actor, histrio – actor
advocatus – lawyer
agricola – farmer
arator – plowman, farmer
arquitectus, artifex – architect
artifex – artist
athleta – athlete
auctor – author

bellator – warrior

caementarius – mason
cantor – singer, musician
caput – boss, leader
collectarius – banker, cashier
cocus, coquus – cook
compuntantis, ratiocinator – bookkeeper

faber – smith, carpenter

iudex – judge

lignarius – carpenter, woodworker
ludio – player

macello, macellarius – butcher
magister – master, teacher
medicus – doctor, physician
mima, mimula – actress
minister – server, servant, minister
musicus – musician
miles/militus – soldier

nauta – sailor

operarius – worker

pastor – shepherd, pastor
physicus – scientist
piscator – fisherman
pictor – painter
pistor – baker, miller
praesidens – president

sacerdos – priest
saltator – dancer
scriba, notarius – secretary, notary
scriptor – writer

venator – hunter

PATRIA (COUNTRIES)

THE VERB *VENIRE* (TO COME)

IN THE PRESENT

ego **venio** – I come
tu **venis** – you come
is/ea **venit** – he/she comes

nos **venimus** – we come
vos **venitis** – you all come
ei/eae **veniunt** – they come

IN THE PERFECT PAST

ego **veni** – I came, have come
tu **venisti** – you came, have come
is/ea **venit** – he/she came, has come

nos **venimus** – we came, have come
vos **venistis** – you all came, have come
ei/eae **venerunt** – they came, have come

Veni, vidi, vici. -Iulius Caesar
I came, I saw, I conquered.

WHERE DO YOU COME FROM?

Unde venisti?
Unde venis?

Where are you from?
Where have you come from?
Where do you come from?

Venio de/Veni de– I come from…

...de terra Germania.
...from Germany.

Germanicus sum.
Teutonicus sum.
I am a German.

Unde venistis?
Unde venitis?
Where do you all come from?

Venimus de – We come from…

Unde venit?
Where does he/she come from?

Venit de...
He/She comes from...

Unde venerunt?
Unde veniunt?
Where do they come from?

Venerunt de...
They come from…

COUNTRIES

Veni de– I come from…

Aegyptus – Egypt

Arabia – Arabia
Brittania – Great Britain
Caledonia – Scotland
Germania – Germany
Graecia/Achaea – Greece
Helvatia – Switzerland
Hibernia – Ireland
Hispania – Spain
Gallia – France
India – India
Israhel/Iudaea – Israel/Judea
Italia – Italy
Libanum – Lebanon
Sina – China
Tunesia – Tunisia

LINGUAE MUNDI (LANGUAGES OF THE WORLD)

THE VERB *LOQUOR* (TO SPEAK)

ego **loquor** – I speak
tu **loqueris** – you speak
is/ea **loquitur** – he/she speaks

nos **loquimur** – we speak
vos **loquimi** – you all speak
ei/eae **loquuntur** – they speak

DO YOU SPEAK LATIN?

Loquerisne* Latine?
Do you speak Latin?

*The suffix -ne is sometimes used at the end of the verb form when asking a question whose answer is "yes" or "no".

Latine nosti?**
Do you speak Latin?

**Literally,

Do you know Latin?

or

Are you familiar with Latin?

LANGUAGES

Loquerisne...?
Do you speak...?

Graece? – Greek?
Anglice? – English?
Italiane? – Italian?
Gallice? – French?
Hispanice? – Spanish?
Iudaice? – Hebrew?
Latine? – Latin?
Theodisce? – German?
Sinice? – Chinese?
Arabice? - Arab?
Persice? – Persian?
Indice? - Hindi?

Intellego.
I understand.

Non intellego.
I don't understand.

Precor ut loquaris lente.
Please, speak more slowly.

URBES (CITIES)

Ubi habitas?
Where do you live?

Romae habito.
I live in Rome.

Ubi habitatis?
Where do you all live?

Athenis habitamus.
We live in Athens.

Ubi habitat?
Where does he/she live?

Corinthi habitat.
He/She lives in Corinth.

Ubi habitant? – Where do they live?

Aurelia Aquensi habitant.
They live in Baden-Baden, Germany.

Urbes mundi
(the cities of the world)

Athenae – Athens
Aurelia Aquensi – Baden-Baden
Carthago – Carthage
Hierosolymum – Jerusalem
Neapoli - Naples
Lacedaemoniis – Sparta
Londinium – London

Roma - Rome
Valentia – Valencia

AETATE (TALKING ABOUT AGE)

Qua aetate es?
How old are you?

Qua aetate estis?
How old are you all?

Qua aetate est?
How old is he/she?

25 annos natus (says a man)
25 annos nata (says a woman)
25 years old

Qua aetate sunt?
How old are they?

aetate – age
adolescens/adulescens – teen/adolescent
adultus – adult

iuvenis – young
iunor - younger

vetus/veteris – old
maior - older

unus – 1
duo – 2
tres – 3
quattuor – 4
cinque – 5
sex – 6

septem – 7
octo – 8
novem – 9
decem – 10

undecim – 11
duodecim – 12
tredecim – 13
quattuordecim – 14
quindecim – 15
sedecim - 16
septendecim – 17
duodeviginti – 18
undeviginti – 19

viginti - 20
vinginti unus - 21
viginti duo, etc. – 22, etc.

triginta – 30
quadraginta – 40
quinquaginta – 50
sextaginta – 60
septuaginta – 70
octoginta – 80
nonaginta – 90

centum – 100

ducenti, *ducentae*, *ducenta* – 200
trecenti, *trecentae*, *trencenta* – 300
quadringenti, *etc.* – 400, etc.
quingenti – 500
sescenti – 600
septignenti – 700

octingenti – 800
nongenti – 900
mille – 1,000
duo milia – 2,000

DIES, MENSIS, ANNI TEMPUS (DAYS, MONTHS, SEASONS)

DAYS OF THE WEEK

Diebus sabbatorum
(Days of the Week)

dies lunae – Monday
dies martis – Tuesday
dies mercurii – Wednesday
dies iovis – Thursday
dies veneris – Friday
dies saturni – Saturday
dies solis – Sunday

MONTHS OF THE YEAR

In mensibus anni
(Months of the Year)

Ianuarius – January
Februarius– February
Martius – March
Abrilis – April
Maius – May
Iunius – June
Iulius – July
Augustus– August
September – September
October– October
November – November

December – December

SEASONS OF THE YEAR

Anni tempus
hiems – winter
tempus vernum – spring
aestes– summer
autumnus – autumn, fall

OTHER WORDS AND PHRASES

hodie – today

hesterno/heri - yesterday
dies ante heri – the day before yesterday

cras – tomorrow
postridie/perendies – the day after tomorrow

haec septimana – this week
ultima septimana – last week
proxima septimana – next week

hic mensis – this month
utlimo mensis – last month
proximo mensis – next month

hic anno – this year
ultimo anno/anno superiore – last year
proximo anno/ad annum – next year

NUMERO (NUMBERS)

unus – 1
duo – 2
tres – 3
quattuor – 4
cinque – 5
sex – 6
septem – 7
octo – 8
novem – 9
decem – 10

undecim – 11
duodecim – 12
tredecim – 13
quattuordecim – 14
quindecim – 15
sedecim - 16
septendecim – 17
duodeviginti – 18
undeviginti – 19

viginti - 20
vinginti unus - 21
viginti duo, etc. – 22, etc.

triginta – 30
quadraginta – 40
quinquaginta – 50
sextaginta – 60
septuaginta – 70
octoginta – 80

nonaginta – 90

centum – 100

ducenti, *ducentae*, *ducenta* – 200
trecenti, *trecentae*, *trencenta* – 300
quadringenti, *etc.* – 400, etc.
quingenti – 500
sescenti – 600
septignenti – 700
octingenti – 800
nongenti – 900
mille – 1,000
duo milia – 2,000

HORA DIEI (THE TIME OF DAY)

Qua hora est?
What time is it?

Prima hora mane est.
It's seven in the morning.

hora diei
(hours of the day)

prima hora – 7:00
secunda hora – 8:00
tertia hora – 9:00
quarta hora – 10:00
quinta hora – 11:00
sexta hora – 12:00
septima hora – 13:00
octava hora – 14:00
nona hora – 15:00
decima hora – 16:00
undecima hora – 17:00
duodecima hora – 18:00

Hours of the Night:

prima vigilia
(first night watch)

hora prima – 19:00
hora secunda – 20:00
hora tertia – 21:00

secunda vigilia
(second night watch)

hora quarta – 22:00
hora quinta – 23:00
hora sexta – 24:00

tertia vigilia
(third night watch)

hora septima – 1:00
hora octava – 2:00
hora nona – 3:00

quarta vigilia
(fourth night watch)

hora decima – 4:00
hora undecima – 5:00
hora duodecima – 6:00

mane – in the morning
ad meridiem – at noon
post meridiem – in the afternoon
ad noctem – in the evening
in nocte ista – this evening
media noctis – at midnight

ACT ONES (ACT V T ES)

ego **amo** – I like
tu **amas** – you like
is/ea **amat** – he/she likes

nos **amamus** – we like
vos **amatis** – you all like
ei/eae **amant** – they like

*literally, "I love"

Amo pingere. – I like to paint.

libentissime – gladly

Pingo libentissime. – I like to paint.
(I paint gladly/I enjoy painting)

ad arenam ire – to go to the arena
ad castra ire – to go camping
ad forum ire – to go to the market
ad navegandum ire – to go sailing
ad theatrum ire – to go to the theater
ambulare – to walk
canere, cantare – to sing
certamen spectare – to watch a game
currere – to run
delineare – to draw, sketch
equitare – to ride horses
exercere – to exercise, train
fabula spectare – to watch a play
legere – to read
musicam audire – to listen to music

natare – to swim
pingere – to paint
ludere – to play
ludere instrumentum
to play a musical instrument
ludos facere – to do sports
saltare – to dance

THE VERBS IRE AND *VADERE* (TO GO)

Present: I go, I am going, I do go

Imperfect Past: I went, I was going, I used to go

Perfect Past: I went, I have gone

Future: I will go

In Latin, there are two different verbs that express the meaning of "to go" in English.

VADERE

IN THE PRESENT

ego **vado** – I go
tu **vadis** – you go
is **vadit** – he goes
nos **vadimus** – we go
vos **vaditis** – you all go
ei **vadunt** – they go

IN THE IMPERFECT PAST

ego **vadebam** – I went, was going
tu **vadebas** – you went, were going
is **vadebat** – he went, was going
nos **vadebamus** – we went, were going
vos **vadebitis** – you all went, were going

ei **vadebant** – they went, were going

IN THE PERFECT PAST

ego **vasi** – I went, have gone
tu **vasisti** – you went, have gone
is **vasit** – he went, has gone
nos **vasimus** – we went, have gone
vos **vasistis** – you all went, have gone
ei **vaserunt** – they went, have gone

IN THE FUTURE

ego **vadam** – I will go
tu **vades** – you will go
is **vadet** – he will go
nos **vademus** – we will go
vos **vadetis** – you all will go
ei **vadent** – they will go

IRE

IN THE PRESENT

ego **eo** – I go
tu **is** – you go
is **it** – he goes
nos **imus** – we go
vos **itis** – you all go
ei **eunt** – they go

IN THE IMPERFECT PAST

ego **ibam** – I went, was going
tu **ibas** – you went, were going
is **ibat** – he went, was going
nos **ibamus** – we went, were going
vos **ibatis** – you all went, were going
ei **ibant** – they went, were going

IN THE PERFECT PAST

ego **ii** – I went, have gone
tu **isti** – you went, have gone
is **iit** – he went, has gone
nos **iimus** – we went, have gone
vos **iistis** – you all went, have gone
ei **ierunt** – they went, have gone

IN THE FUTURE

ego **ibo** – I will go
tu **ibis** – you will go
is **ibit** – he will go
nos **ibiamus** – we will go
vos **ibitis** – you all will go
ei **ibunt** – they will go

LOCIS (PLACES)

WHERE ARE YOU GOING?

Quo vadis?
Where are you going?

Vado... – I'm going…

Quo vaditis?
Where are you all going?

Vadimus... – We're going...

Quo vadit? – Where is he going?

Vadit... – He's going...

Quo vadunt?
Where are they going?

Vadunt... – They're going…

PLACES AND PREPOSITIONAL PHRASES

ad **detrix** – at the right (side)
ad **dexteram** – on the right hand
ad **ianuam** – at the door, to the door
ad **locum** – to a place
ad **mare** – to the sea(side), by the seaside
ad **montem** – to the mountain
ad **sinistram** – on the left hand
ad **vesperam** – in the evening

circa **mare** – near the sea, by the seaside

circa **viam** – by the way(side), near the way

in **agro** – in the field
in agris – in the fields
in **caelo**/in **caelis** – in the sky, in heaven
in **caelum** – up to(wards) heaven, the sky
in **carcere** – in jail, in prison
in **castella** – into the towns
in **civitate** – in the city (of)
in civitatem – to the city
in **deserto** – in the desert
in desertum – to the desert, into the desert
in **disco** – in a dish, on a platter
in **diversorio** – in the inn, hotel
in **domo** – in/at the house
domi – at home, in one's own country
in domum – (in)to the house (of), to home
et si dimisero eos ieiunos in domum suam – and if I will send them to their homes
in **foro** – at the market
in **flumine** – in the river
in **furorem versus** – mad, crazy, beside onself, out of one's mind
in **gradibus** – in the stairs/steps
in **ieiunio** – fasting, by fasting
in **ignem** – into the fire
in **loco** – in a place, in the place
in locum – into a place
in locis – in places
in **mari** – in the sea
in **medio eorum** – in the midst of them, in their midst
in **medium** – in the middle, in the midst
in **monte**(m) – in(to) the mountain
in **monumento** – in a tomb

in **navem** – into the ship
in **navi** – in the ship
in **nocte ista** – this night, tonight, this evening
in **nomine** – in the name of
in nomine meo – in my name
in **nullo** – in nothing, by nothing
in **oratione** – in prayer, by prayer
in **principio** – in the beginning
in **sinagoga** – in the synagogue
in **solitudine** – in the wilderness, in the middle of nowhere
in **tabernaculo** – in the tent
in **terra** – on earth, on land
in **toto** – in entirety
in **utero** – in the womb
ex utero – from birth
in **vanum** – in vain
in **ventrum** – into the stomach, belly
in **via** – in the way, on the way, along the way
in **vicum** – into the town
in **virtute** – in power

inter **vos** – amongst yourselves

retro **me** – behind me
Vade retro me, Satana! – Get behind me, Satan!

sub **mensa** – under the table

super **faenum** – on the grass
super viride faenum – upon the green grass
super **terra** – upon land, on dry land

supra **lectum** – on the bed, in the bed

MANDUCARE ET BIBERE (EATING AND DRINKING)

FRUCTUS (FRUIT)

arantium – orange
carica – fig
cerasus – cherry
cucumis – melon
dactylus – date
ficus – fig, fig tree
malum/pomum – apple
malum punicum – pomegranate
persicum – peach
pirum – pear
uva – grape
uva passa – raisin

HOLUS (VEGETABLE)

allium – garlic
brassica – cabbage, brussel sprout
cepa – onion
cucumis (n.) – cucumber
cucurbita – squash, pumpkin
cucurbitula – zucchini, courgette
(h)olus (n^3) – vegetable
lactuca – lettuce
legumen, *leguminis* (n^3) – beans, legumes

oliva – olive

CARNIS (MEAT)

anatina – duck meat
agnus – lamb
bubula – beef
farcimen, *farciminis* (n.) – sausage
iecur, *iecoris* (n.) – liver
piscis (m.) – fish
pullus – chicken
porcina – pork
vitulina – veal

MISCELLUS (MISCELLANEOUS)

acetarium, acetaria (pl.) – salad
acetum – vinegar
ampulla – bottle
aqua – water

bibo, bibere – to drink

calix, *calicis* (m³) – cup, glass, chalice
cervisia – beer
caseus – cheese
cena – dinner, supper
incenare – to have dinner, supper
clibanus/fornus – oven
comedo, comedere – to eat
coclear – spoon
culter – knife

farina – flour
furca – fork

hydria – jug, pitcher

ius, *iuris* (n.) – broth, soup

lac, *lactis* (n.) – milk

manduco, manducare – to eat
massa – mass, lump, cake, nugget
mel, *mellis* (n.) – honey
mensa – table
oleum– oil
ova (n. pl.) – eggs
ovum (n.) – egg

pane, *panis* (n.) – bread
patella – small plate, saucer
piper, *piperis* (m) – pepper
prandium – meal
pulmente/pulmentum – soup, stew

sal, *salis* (m.) – salt
sinapis (f [3]) – mustard
sucus – juice

vinum – wine

EXAMPLE SENTENCES

Favus distillans labia tua sponsa mel et lac sub lingua tua et odor vestimentorum tuorum sicut odor turis.

Your lips, my bride, are like a honeycomb, honey and milk are under your tongue, and the fragrance of your clothes is like frankincense.

Guttur tuum sicut vinum optimum dignum dilecto meo ad potandum labiisque et dentibus illius ruminandum.

Your mouth (throat) like the best wine for my beloved to drink and for the lips and teeth to savor.

Veniat dilectus meus in hortum suum et comedat fructum pomorum suorum. Veni in hortum meum soror mea sponsa messui murram meam cum aromatibus meis. Comedi favum cum melle meo, bibi vinum meum cum lacte meo. Comedite amici bibite et inebriamini carissimi

Let my lover come to his garden and eat the fruits of his apple trees. I came to my garden, O my sister, my bride, I collected my myrrh with my aromatic spices. I ate the honeycomb with my honey, I drank my wine with my milk: Eat and drink and be drunk, my dearest friends!

- *Vulgate* (Song of Solomon)

Et invenerunt virum aegyptium in agro et adduxerunt eum ad David dederuntque ei panem ut comederet et ut biberet aquam, sed et fragmen massae caricarum et duas ligaturas uvae passae quae cum comedisset reversus est spiritus eius et refocilatus est non enim comederat panem neque biberat aquam tribus diebus et tribus noctibus

And they found an Egyptian in the field and brought him to David; and they gave him bread to eat and water to drink, and also a piece of cake with figs and two clusters of raisins. And when he had eaten them, his spirit returned, and he was refreshed; for he had neither eaten bread nor drunk water, three days and three nights.

- *Vulgate* (1 Samuel, 30: 11, 12)

Corvi quoque deferebant panem et carnes mane similiter panem et carnes vesperi et bibebat de torrente.

And the ravens brought him bread and meat in the morning and bread and meat in the evening; and he drank from the stream. – Vulgate, 1 Kings 17: 6

Quae respondit vivit Dominus Deus tuus quia non habeo panem nisi quantum pugillus capere potest farinae in hydria et paululum olei in lecytho en colligo duo ligna ut ingrediar et faciam illud mihi et filio meo ut comedamus et moriamur.

And she answered: As the Lord your God lives, I have no bread, but only a handful of flour in a pot and a little oil in a jar. You can see that I am collecting two sticks so I can go in and prepare it. for me and my son to eat and then we will die.

- *Vulgate*, 1Kings 17:12)

POPULUM DESCRIBERE (DESCRIBING PEOPLE)

WHAT DOES HE LOOK LIKE?

Magnus est.
Altus est.
He is big.
He is tall.

Parva est.
She is small.
She is short.

Pulcher est.
He is handsome.

Pulchra est.
She is pretty.

Pulchri sunt.
They are handsome. (m.)

Pulchrae sunt.
They are pretty (f.)

altus – tall
magnus – big, large, great

parvus – small, short
tenius – thin
crassus - fat

pulcher – lovely, attractive

deformis, turpis – ugly

serius, gravis – serious, severe
iocosus/comicus – funny
festivus – fun, enjoyable

intelligens – intelligent
novus, iucundus – interesting
odiosis, molestus, longinquus – boring

iucundus – agreeable, pleasant
iniudundus – unpleasant
amicus – nice, friendly
comis, urbanus – polite
rudis – rude, impolite

industrius, sedulus – hardworking
otiosus, tiger, iners – lazy

sufflavaus, subflavus - blond
brunus, brunetus – brown-haired
rufus – red-haired, ruddy

felix – happy
contentus – content

tristis – sad
pusillanimis – discouraged
depressus – depressed

turbatus – irritated
iratus – angry

trepidus/pavidus – afraid, frightened
anxius, sollicitus – worried

nervosus, trepidus, timidis – nervous

placidus – calm, tranquil

lassus/defussus – tired
infirmus, malus – sick, ill

ADJECTIVE LIST (LATIN/ENGLISH)

altus – tall
amicus – nice
anxius, sollicitus – worried
brunus, brunetus – brown-haired
comis, urbanus – polite
contentus – content
crassus – fat
deformis, turpis – ugly
depressus – depressed
felix – happy
festivus – fun, enjoyable
industrius, sedulus – hardworking
infirmus, malus – sick, ill
iniudundus – unpleasant
intelligens - intelligent
iocosus/comicus – funny
iratus – angry
iucundus – agreeable, pleasant
lassus/defussus – tired
magnus – big, large, great
nervosus, trepidus, timidis – nervous
novus, iucundus – interesting
odiosis, molestus, longinquus – boring
otiosus, tiger, iners – lazy
parvus – small, short in stature
placidus – calm, tranquil

pulcher – lovely, attractive
pusillanimis – discouraged
rudis – rude, impolite
rufus – red-haired, ruddy
serius, gravis – serious
sufflavaus, subflavus – blond
tenius – thin
trepidus/pavidus – afraid, frightened
tristis – sad
turbatus – irritated

CORPUS (THE BODY)

auris (f.) – ear
barba – beard
brachium – arm
calvaria – skull, cranium
capillus – hair
caput, capitis (n.) – head
cerebrum– brain
collum – neck
cor, *cordis* (n.) – heart
coxa – hip
crus, *cruris* (n.) – leg
digitus – finger
dens, *dentis* (m.) – tooth
facies (f.) – face
faux, *faucis, fauces* (f.)– larynx, throat
femur (n.) – thigh
frons, *frontis* (f.) – forehead
gena – cheek
genu, *genus* (n.) – knee
gutter, *gutteris* (n.) – throat

humerus/umerus – shoulder
iecur, *iecinoris* (n.) – liver
labrum – lip
lingua – tongue
mandíbula/maxilla – jaw
manus (f.) – hand
mens, *mentis* (f.) – mind
mentum – chin
musculus – muscle
nasus – nose
os, *oris* (n.) – mouth
os, *ossis* (n.) – bone
oculus – eye
pellis (f.) – skin
pes, *pedis* (m.) – foot
pectus, *pectis* (n.) – chest, breast
pulmo, *pulmonis* (m.) – lung
pupilla – pupil
ren, renis, renes (m.) – kidney
saliva – saliva, spit(tle)
sanguis (m.) – blood
scapula – shoulder blade(s), back
spina – spine
umbilicus – navel
vena – vein
venter, *ventris* (m.) – stomach

EXAMPLE SENTENCES

Pulchrae sunt genae tuae sicut turturis collum tuum sicut monilia. Your cheeks are lovely as turtle doves, your neck like precious jewels.

Vulnerasti cor meum soror mea sponsa vulnerasti cor meum in uno oculorum tuorum et in uno crine colli tui.

You have ravished my heart, my sister, my bride, you have ravished my heart with one of your eyes and one chain (curl) of your neck.

Favus distillans labia tua sponsa mel et lac sub lingua tua et odor vestimentorum tuorum sicut odor turis.

Your lips, my bride, are like a honeycomb, honey and milk are under your tongue, and the fragrance of your clothes is like frankincense.

Manus illius tornatiles aureae plenae hyacinthis. Venter eius eburneus distinctus sapphyris.

His hands are turned and like gold, full of hyacinths. His belly is like ivory, set with sapphires.

Crura illius columnae marmoreae quae fundatae sunt super bases aureas. Species eius ut Libani electus ut cedri

His legs as marble pillars resting on gold bases. Their shape like Lebanon, excellent as the cedars.

Collum tuum sicut turris eburnea. Oculi tui sicut piscinae in Esebon quae sunt in porta filiae multitudinis. Nasus tuus sicut turris Libani quae respicit contra Damascum.

Your neck as a tower of ivory. Your eyes like the pools in Heshbon, by the gate of *Bath-rabbim* (lit. *daughter of the multitudes*). Your nose is like the tower of Lebanon looking towards Damascus.

Guttur tuum sicut vinum optimum dignum dilecto meo ad potandum labiisque et dentibus illius ruminandum.

Your mouth (throat) like the best wine for my beloved to drink and for the lips and teeth to savor.

- *Vulgate* (Song of Solomon)

Erat autem rufus et pulcher aspectu decoraque facie.

He had a ruddy (reddish) complexion and was handsome in appearance and face.

Et cassis aerea super caput eius et lorica hamata induebatur porro pondus loricae eius quinque milia siclorum aeris. Et ocreas aereas habebat in cruribus et clypeus aereus tegebat umeros eius.

And he had a brass helmet on his head, and he was clothed in a shirt of mail, and the weight of his armor coat was five thousand sicles of brass: and he had brass greaves on his legs, and a brass shield slung over his shoulders.

- *Vulgate* (2 Samuel)

COLORES (COLORS)

albus – white
arantius – orange
aureus – golden
brun(i)us – brown
caerul(e)us/azureus – blue
flavus – yellow
griseus – gray/grey
niger – black
purpura – purple
roseus – pink
ruber – red
rubicundus – red, reddish
veridis – green

candidus – light
obscurus – dark

Malum rubrum est.
The apple is red.

Pirum veridis est.
The pear is green.

Uvae purpurae sunt.
The grapes are purple.

Nubes grisea est.
The cloud is gray.

Caelum azureum est.
The sky is blue.

Equus niger est.

The horse is black.

IN DOMO (AT HOME)

Mensa magna est.
The table is big.

Mensae magnae sunt.
The tables are big.

Fenestra parva est.
The window is small.

Fenestra non magna est.
The window isn't big.

Sellae pulchrae sunt.
The chairs are pretty.

cathedra – seat, place, chair
cena – supper, dinner
cenaculum – upper room, garret
cubiculum – bedroom, bed
cubitus – bed, sofa
clavis – key
culina – kitchen
fenestra – window
grabatus – cot, campbed
hortus – garden
lampas/lucerna - lamp
lectulus – sofa, couch
lectus – bed
mensa – table
ostium – door
porticus/vestibulum – porch, vestibule
recubitus – eating room or couch*

scalae/scalaria/tribunalis – stair(s)
sella – chair, seat, place
sera – lock
sessorium – living room
solarium – balcony
speculum – mirror
tapete – carpet, rug
trinclinium – dining room

Amant autem primos recubitus in cenis et primas cathedras.
And they love the first places* and the first seats at the dinners.

Vulgate, Matt. 23:6

*or "place of honor," The word "recubitus" comes from the verb "recubare" meaning lie down and probably refers to the usual practice of this era of eating at a low table while lying on the floor.

Et ambulabat Iesus in templo in porticu Salomonis
And Jesus was walking in the temple in Solomon's Porch.

-*Vulgate*, John 10:23

Ego sum ostium per me si quis introierit salvabitur et ingredietur et egredietur et pascua inveniet.

I am the door. If anyone enters by me, he will be saved and will go in and out and find pasture.

Vulgate, John 10:9

Sedens autem quidam adulescens nomine Eutychus super fenestram cum mergeretur somno gravi disputante diu Paulo eductus somno cecidit de tertio cenaculo deorsum et sublatus est mortuus.

And a young man named Eutychus was sitting in a window and fell asleep while Paul was preaching and fell from the third floor of an upper room and was taken up dead.

-*Vulgate*, Acts 20:9

TEMPESTAS (THE WEATHER)

fulgur, fulmen – lightning
nimbus – rainstorm, raincloud
nix, *nivis* – snow
nubes, *nubis* – cloud
nubila – clouds
pluvia – rain
sol, solis – sun
tempestas – storm, weather
tonitrus – thunder
ventus – wind

Quomodo est tempestas?
How is the weather?

Frigus est. – It's cold.
Calidus est.. – It's hot.
Aestus est. – It's really hot.
Serenum est. – It's nice weather.
Ventosus est. – It's windy.
Nubilosus est. – It's foggy.
Nubilis esto. – It's cloudy.

Ningit (multum). – It snows (a lot).
Pluerit (multum). – It rains (lot).

Post dies autem siccatus est torrens non enim pluerat super terram
After some days, the stream dried up, because it had not rained over the land.
-*Vulgate*, (1 Kings 17:7)

Ecce, caeli contenebrati sunt et nubes et ventus et facta est pluvia grandis ascendens.
And behold, the sky became dark with clouds and wind, and there was heavy rain.
-*Vulgate*, (1 Kings 18:45)

Facto vespere dicitis: "Serenum erit rubicundum est enim caelum". Et mane dicitis: "Hodie tempestas rutilat enim triste caelum".

In in the evening you all say: "It will be nice weather because the sky is red".
And in the morning you say: "It will be stormy today because the sky is red and ominous (literally *sad*)".– *Vulgate*, Matt. 16:3

Dicebat autem et ad turbas: Cum videritis nubem ab occasu statim dicitis nimbus venit et ita fit. Et cum austrum flantem dicitis quia aestus erit et fit.

And he said to the multitudes: And when you all see a cloud rising from the west, immediately you say 'A shower is coming', and so it is". And when you see a hot wind coming from the south, you say, 'It will be hot', and so it is".-*Vulgate*, Luke 12:54-55

Et facta est pluvia super terram quadraginta diebus et quadraginta noctibus.
And it rained for 40 days and 40 nights over the earth.

-*Vulgate*, Genesis 7:12

ANIMALA (ANIMALS)

...video – I see...
...videre possum. – I can see...

Avem video.
I see a bird.
I see the bird.

Avem videre possum.
I can see a bird.
I can see the bird.

Musca magna est.
The fly is big.

Muscae magnae sunt.
The flies are big.

Aranea nigra est.
The spider is black.

Aranea nigrae sunt.
The spiders are black.

anas, *anatis* – duck
agnus – lamb
apis – bee
aranea – spider
aries – ram
avem – bird
balaena, balena – whale
bos, *bovis* – ox, cow, bull
caper, *capri* – male goat
capra – female goat

canis – dog
cancer – crab
cattus/felis – cat
corvus – crow, raven
crocodilus – crocodile
elephantus – elephant
equus – horse
formica – ant
gallina – hen
gallus – cockerel, rooster
grex, *gregis* – herd, flock (sheep)
lepus – rabbit, hare
lacerta – lizard
leo, *leonis* – lion
lupus – wolf
mus/musculus – mouse, rat
musca – fly
ovium – sheep
piscis – fish
pullus – chicken
porcus – pig
rana – frog
serpens – snake, serpent
taurus/bos – bull, ox
tigris – tiger
ursus – bear
vacca/bos – cow, ox
volpes, *volpis* – fox

Corvi quoque deferebant panem et carnes mane similiter panem et carnes vesperi et bibebat de torrente.

And the raven brought him bread and meat in the morning and bread and meat in the evening, and he drank from the stream.

-*Vulgate*, (1 King 17:6)

Dixitque David ad Saul pascebat servus tuus patris sui gregem et veniebat leo vel ursus tollebatque arietem de medio gregis.

And David said to Saul: "Your servant used to tend his father's sheep (flock), and when a lion or bear would come to take a lamb from the flock…"

-*Vulgate*, Samuel 17: 34

NATURA (NATURE)

...video – I see...
...videre possum. – I can see...

Montem video.
I see a mountain.
I see the mountain.

Montem videre possum.
I can see a mountain.
I can see the mountain.

aqua – water
arena/harena – sand
arbor – tree
collis – hill
folium – leaf
flumen – river
glacies – ice
herba – grass
lacus/mare – lake
luna – moon
mare – sea
mons, *montis* – mount(ain)
nix – snow
nubis – cloud
nebula – fog
pascuum – pasture
pluviam – rain
pruina/gelu – frost
silva – forest, wood(s)
sol, solis – sun

stella – star
torrens, *torrentis* – stream

Corvi quoque deferebant panem et carnes mane similiter panem et carnes vesperi et bibebat de torrente.
Post dies autem siccatus est torrens non enim pluerat super terram.

And the raven brought him bread and meat in the morning and bread and meat in the evening, and he drank from the stream.

And after some days the stream dried up, because it had not rained over the land.
-*Vulgate*, (1Kings 17: 6, 7)

Ego sum ostium per me si quis introierit salvabitur et ingredietur et egredietur et pascua inveniet.

I am the door. If anyone enters by me, he will be saved, and he will go in and out and find pasture.

-*Vulgate*, John 10:9

TABLES

VERBS

Present: I *love*
Future: I *will love*
Imperfect Past: I *loved, I was loving*
Perfect Past: I *loved, I have loved*

amare (love)	**videre** (see)	**bibere** (drink)
First Conjugation	Second Conjugation	Third Conjugation
Present	**Present**	**Present**
amo	video	bibo
amas	vides	bibis
amat	videt	bibit
amamus	videmus	bibimus
amatis	videtis	bibitis
amant	vident	bibunt

First Conjugation	Second Conjugation	Third Conjugation
Future	**Future**	**Future**
amabo	videbo	bibam
amabis	videbis	bibes
amabit	videbit	bibet
amabimus	videbimus	bibemus
amabatis	videbitis	bibetis
amabunt	videbunt	bibent

First Conjugation	Second Conjugation	Third Conjugation
Imperfect	**Imperfect**	**Imperfect**
amabam	videbam	bibebam
amabas	videbas	bibebas

amabat	videbat	bibebat
amabamus	videbamus	bibebamus
amabatis	videbatis	bibebatis
amabant	videbant	bibebunt

First Conjugation	Second Conjugation	Third Conjugation*
Perfect	**Perfect**	**Perfect**
amavi	vidi	bibi
amavisti	vidisti	bibisti
amavit	vidit	bibit
amavimus	vidimus	bibimus
amavastis	vidistis	bibistis
amaverunt	viderunt	biberunt

The following verbs in the Third Conjugation have an irregular stem in the Perfect:

dicere (to say)→*dix-*
ducere (to lead) →*dux-*
currere (to run) →*cucurr-*
scribere (to write) → *scrips-*
vivere (to live) →*vix-*

facere (do, make)	**audire** (hear)
Third Conj. with -io	Fourth Conjugation
Present	**Present**
facio	audio
facis	audis
facit	audit
facimus	audimus
facitis	auditis
faciunt	audiunt

Third Conj with -io	Fourth Conjugation
Future	**Future**
faciam	audiam
facies	audies
faciet	audiet
faciemus	audiemus
facietis	audietis
facient	audient

Third Conj. with -io	Fourth Conjugation
Imperfect	**Imperfect**
faciebam	audiebam
faciebas	audiebas
faciebat	audiebat
faciebamus	audiebamus
faciebatis	audiebatis
faciebant	audiebant

Third Conj. with -io	Fourth Conjugation
Perfect	**Perfect**
feci	audivi
fecisti	audivisti
fecitt	audivit
fecimus	audivimus
fecistis	audivistis
fecerunt	audiverunt

ADJECTIVES

THE FIRST AND SECOND DECLENSIONS

novus (new)
SINGULAR

Case	M	F	N
Nom	novus	nova	novum
Gen	novi	novae	novi
Dat	novo	novae	novo
Acc	novum	novam	novum
Abl	novo	nova	novo
Voc	nove	nova	novum

PLURAL

Case	M	F	N
Nom	novi	novae	nova
Gen	novorum	novarum	novorum
Dat	novis	novis	novis
Acc	novos	novas	nova
Abl	novis	novis	novis
Voc	novi	novae	nova

liber (free)
SINGULAR

Case	M	F	N
Nom	liber	libera	liberum
Gen	liberi	liberae	liberi
Dat	libero	liberae	libero
Acc	liberum	liberam	liberum
Abl	libero	libera	libero

| Voc | libere | libera | liberum |

PLURAL

Case	M	F	N
Nom	liberi	liberae	libera
Gen	liberorum	liberarum	liberorum
Dat	liberis	liberis	liberis
Acc	liberos	liberas	libera
Abl	liberis	liberis	liberis
Voc	liberi	liberae	libera

pulcher (beautifuly, attractive)

SINGULAR

Case	M	F	N
Nom	pulcher	pulchra	pulchrum
Gen	pulchri	pulchrae	pulchri
Dat	pulchro	pulchrae	puclro
Acc	pulcherum	pulchram	pulchrum
Abl	pulchro	pulchra	pulchro
Voc	pulchre	pulchra	pulchrum

PLURAL

Case	M	F	N
Nom	pulchri	pulchrae	pulchra
Gen	pulchrorum	pulchrarum	pulchrorum
Dat	pulchris	pulchris	pulchris
Acc	pulchros	pulchras	pulchra
Abl	pulchris	pulchris	pulchris
Voc	pulchri	pulchrae	pulchra

THE THIRD DECLENSION

SINGULAR

Case	M	F	N
Nom	Masculine Form	Feminine Form	Neuter Form
Gen	-is	-is	-is
Dat	-i	-i	-i
Acc	-em	-em	Neuter Form
Abl	-i	-i	-i
Voc	Masculine Form	Feminine Form	Neuter Form

PLURAL

Case	M	F	N
Nom	-es	-es	-ia
Gen	-ium	-ium	-ium
Dat	-ibus	-ibus	-ibus
Acc	-es	-es	-ia
Abl	-ibus	-ibus	-ibus
Voc	-es	-es	-ia

felix (happy)
SINGULAR

Case	M	F	N
Nom	felix	felix	felix
Gen	felicis	felicis	felicis
Dat	felici	felici	felici
Acc	felicem	felicem	felix
Abl	felici	felici	felici
Voc	felix	felix	felix

PLURAL

Case	M	F	N
Nom	felices	felices	felicia
Gen	felicium	felicium	felicium
Dat	felicibus	felicibus	felicibus
Acc	felices	felices	felicia
Abl	felicibus	felicibus	felicibus
Voc	felices	felices	felicia

ADJECTIVES LIKE SOLUS

solus (alone, only)

SINGULAR

Case	M	F	N
Nom	solus	sola	solum
Gen	solius	solius	solius
Dat	soli	soli	soli
Acc	solum	solam	solum
Abl	solo	sola	solo
Voc	sole	sola	solum

PLURAL

Case	M	F	N
Nom	soli	solae	sola
Gen	solorum	solarum	solorum
Dat	solis	solis	solis
Acc	solos	solas	sola
Abl	solis	solis	solis
Voc	soli	solae	sola

Here are other adjectives like "solus"

alius – other
alterus – (an)other (between two)
neuter – neither
nullus – none
totus – whole, entire, all
ullus – any
unus – one

uter – either (of two)

FELIX AND POTENS

felix (happy)

SINGULAR

Case	M	F	N
Nom	felix	felix	felix
Gen	felicis	felicis	felicis
Dat	felici	felici	felici
Acc	felicem	felicem	felix
Abl	felici	felici	felici
Voc	felix	felix	felix

PLURAL

Case	M	F	N
Nom	felices	felices	felicia
Gen	felicium	felicium	felicium
Dat	felicibus	felicibus	felicibus
Acc	felices	felices	felicia
Abl	felicibus	felicibus	felicibus
Voc	felices	felices	felicia

potens (powerful)

SINGULAR

Case	M	F	N
Nom	potens	potens	potens
Gen	potentis	potentis	potentis
Dat	potenti	potenti	potenti
Acc	potentem	potentem	potens
Abl	potenti	potenti	potenti
Voc	potens	potens	potens

PLURAL

Case	M	F	N
Nom	potentes	potentes	potentia
Gen	potentium	potentium	potentium
Dat	potentibus	potentibus	potentibus
Acc	potentes	potentes	potentia
Abl	potentibus	potentibus	potentibus
Voc	potentes	potentes	potentia

Printed in Great Britain
by Amazon